SKETCH31 PEN & MARKER

31 DAYS OF DRAWINGS

MIKE CRESSY

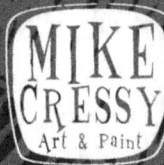

©COPYRIGHT 2020

SKETCH31

This is Volume one of SKETCH31 Pen and Marker.

All rights reserved. No part of this publication my be reproduced, distributed or transmitted in any form or by any means, including photocopying, recording or other electronic or mechanical methods of reproduction
without the prior expressed permission of Mike Cressy.

Names, characters, places and scenarios featured in this publication are fictitious and any resemblance to real persons living or dead, events or institutions or localities are purely coincidental.

Layout and design by Mike Cressy

Visit my portfolio at: https://www.pinterest.com/mikecressy/

ISBN: 9781651922705

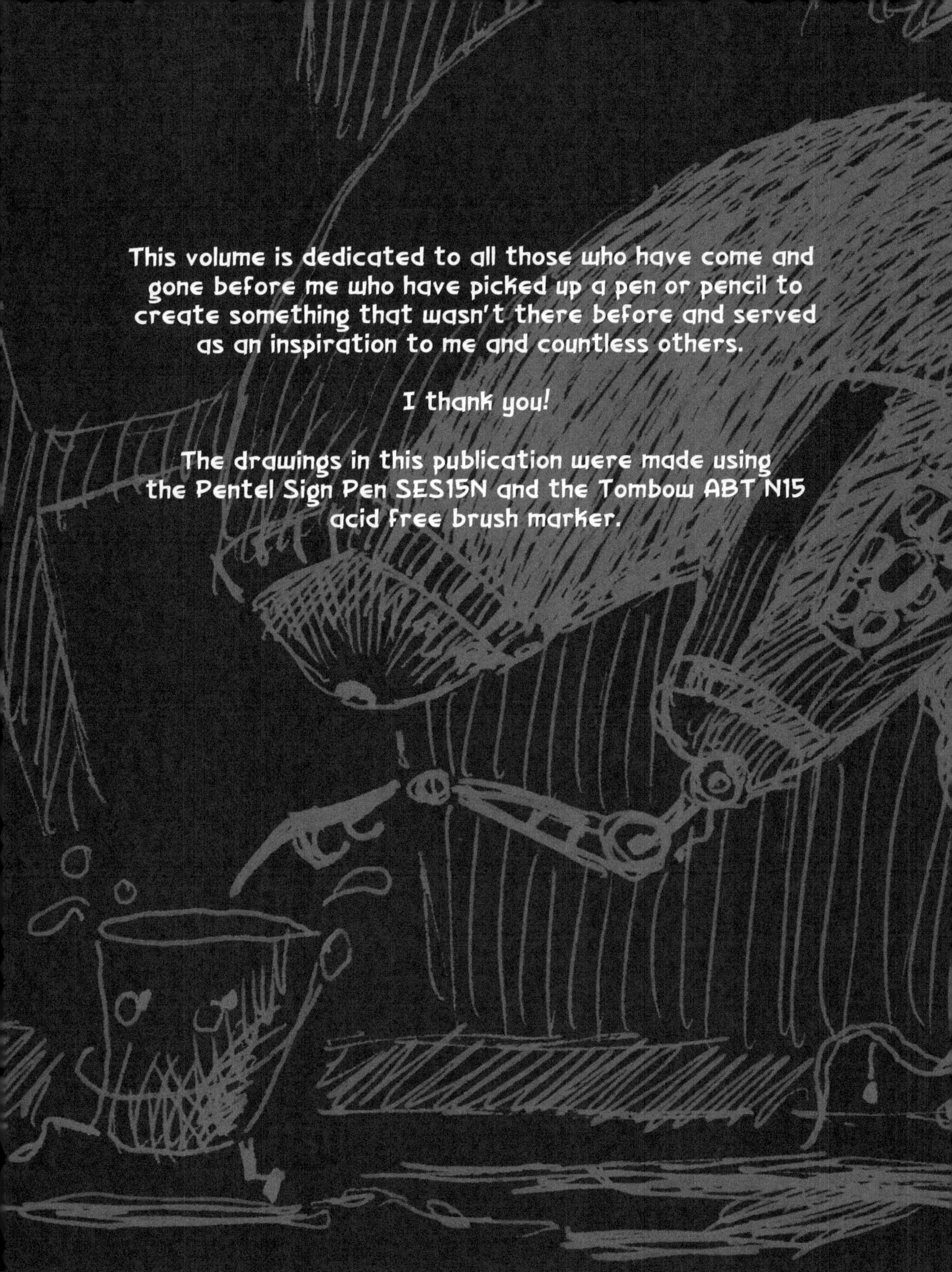

This volume is dedicated to all those who have come and gone before me who have picked up a pen or pencil to create something that wasn't there before and served as an inspiration to me and countless others.

I thank you!

The drawings in this publication were made using the Pentel Sign Pen SES15N and the Tombow ABT N15 acid free brush marker.

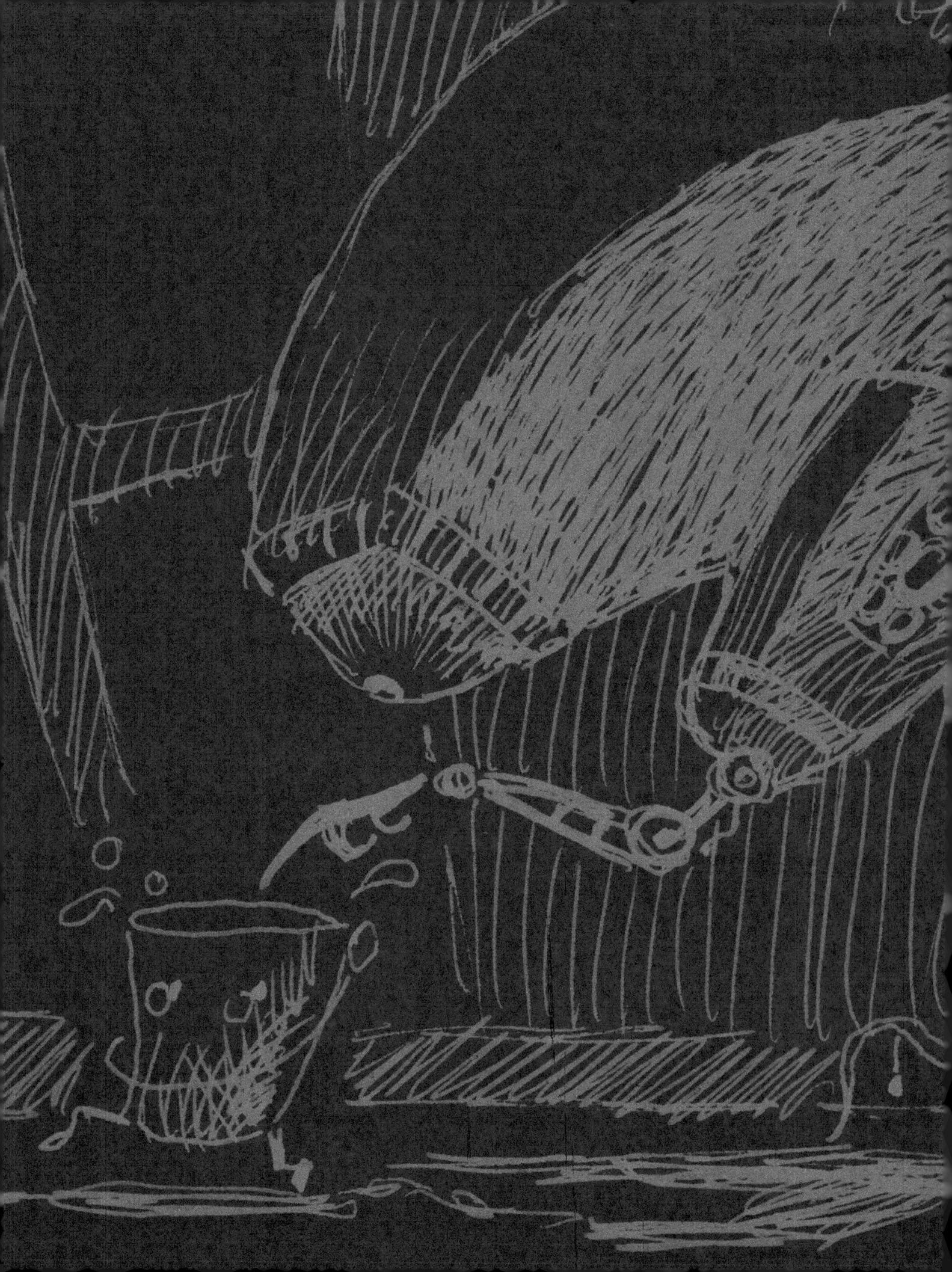

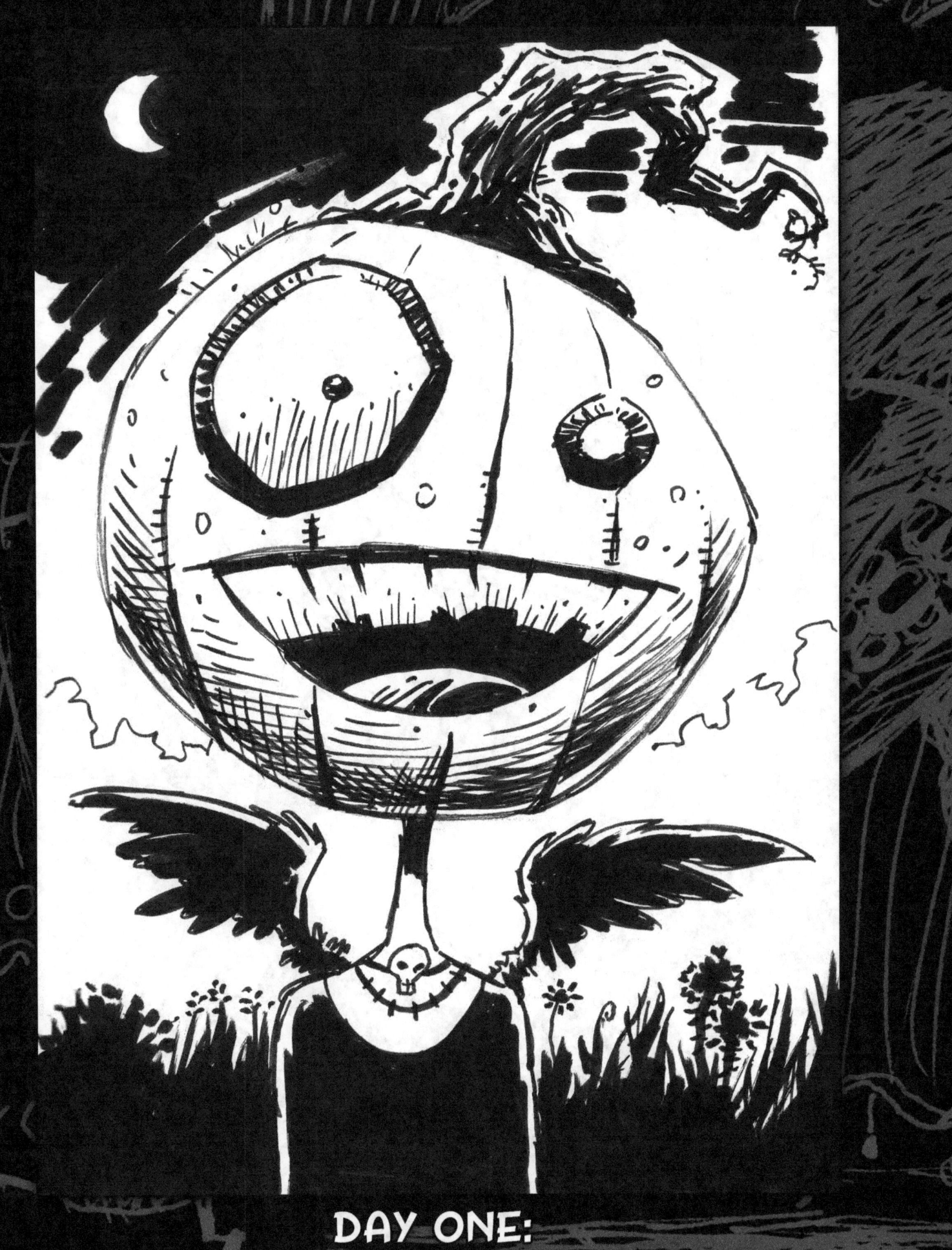

**DAY ONE:
PUMPKIN HEAD ARRIVES**

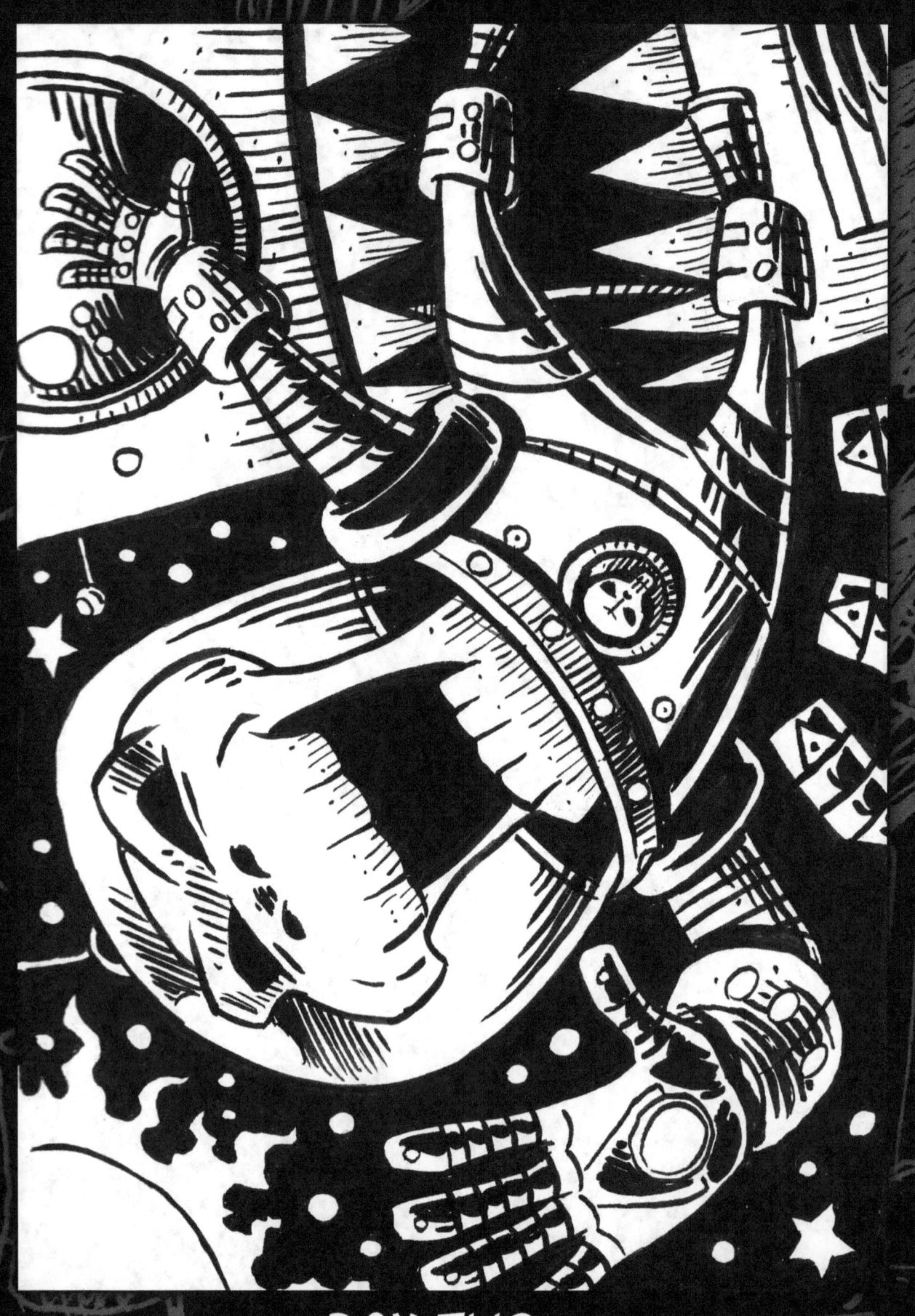

DAY TWO:
SPACE SKULL ESCAPES

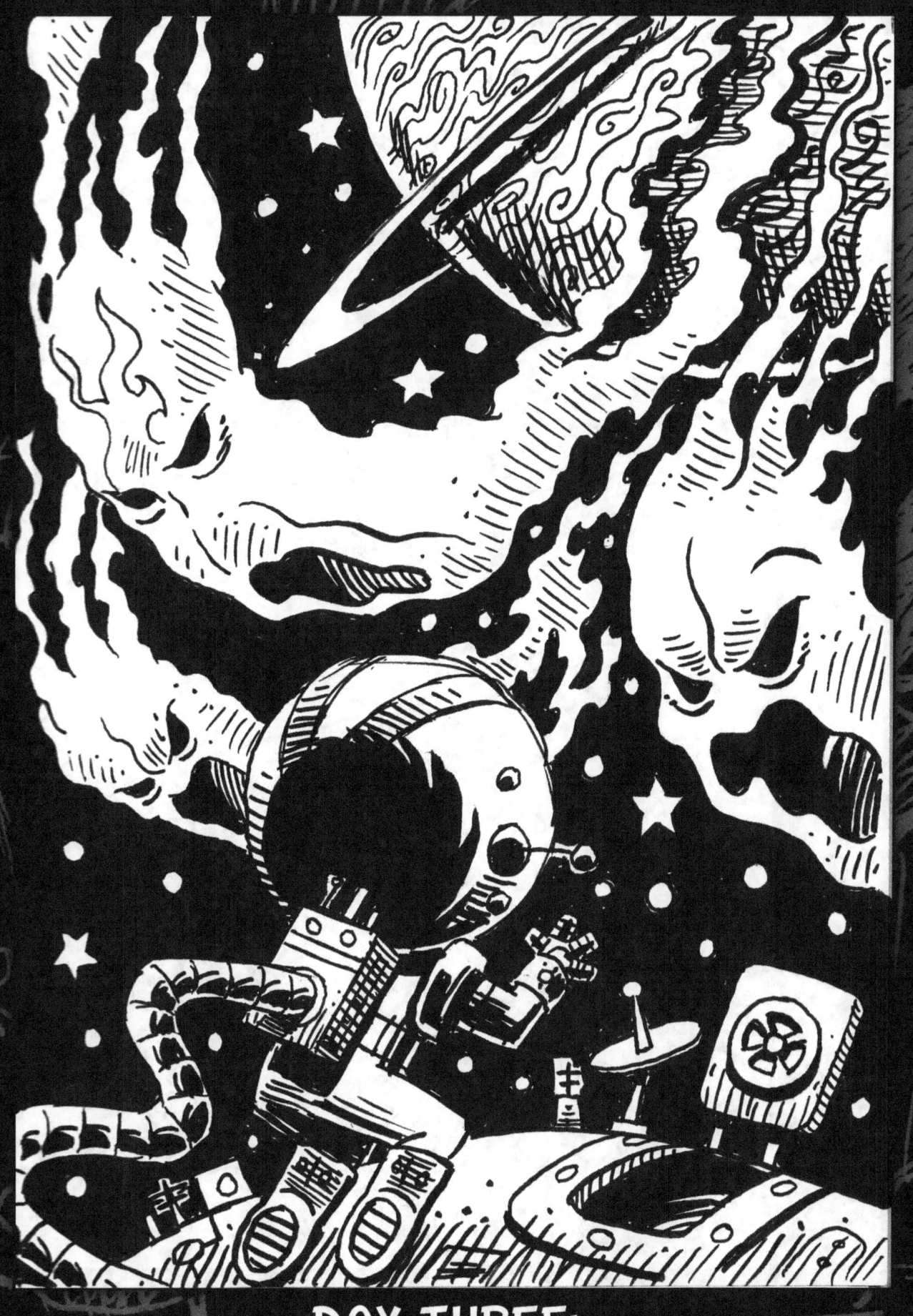

DAY THREE:
SPACE GHOSTS ATTACK

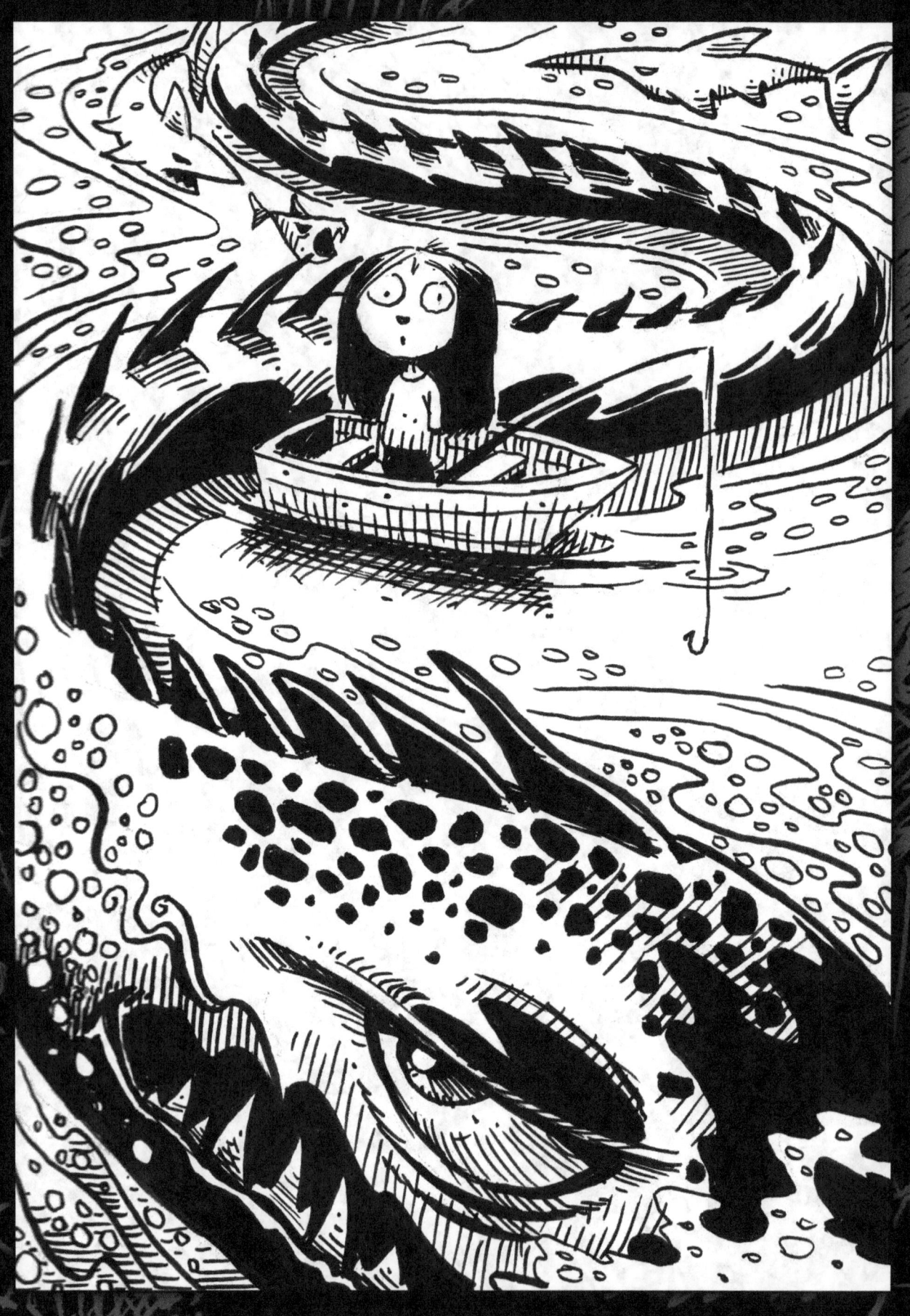

DAY FOUR:
FISHING JUST GOT DIFFICULT

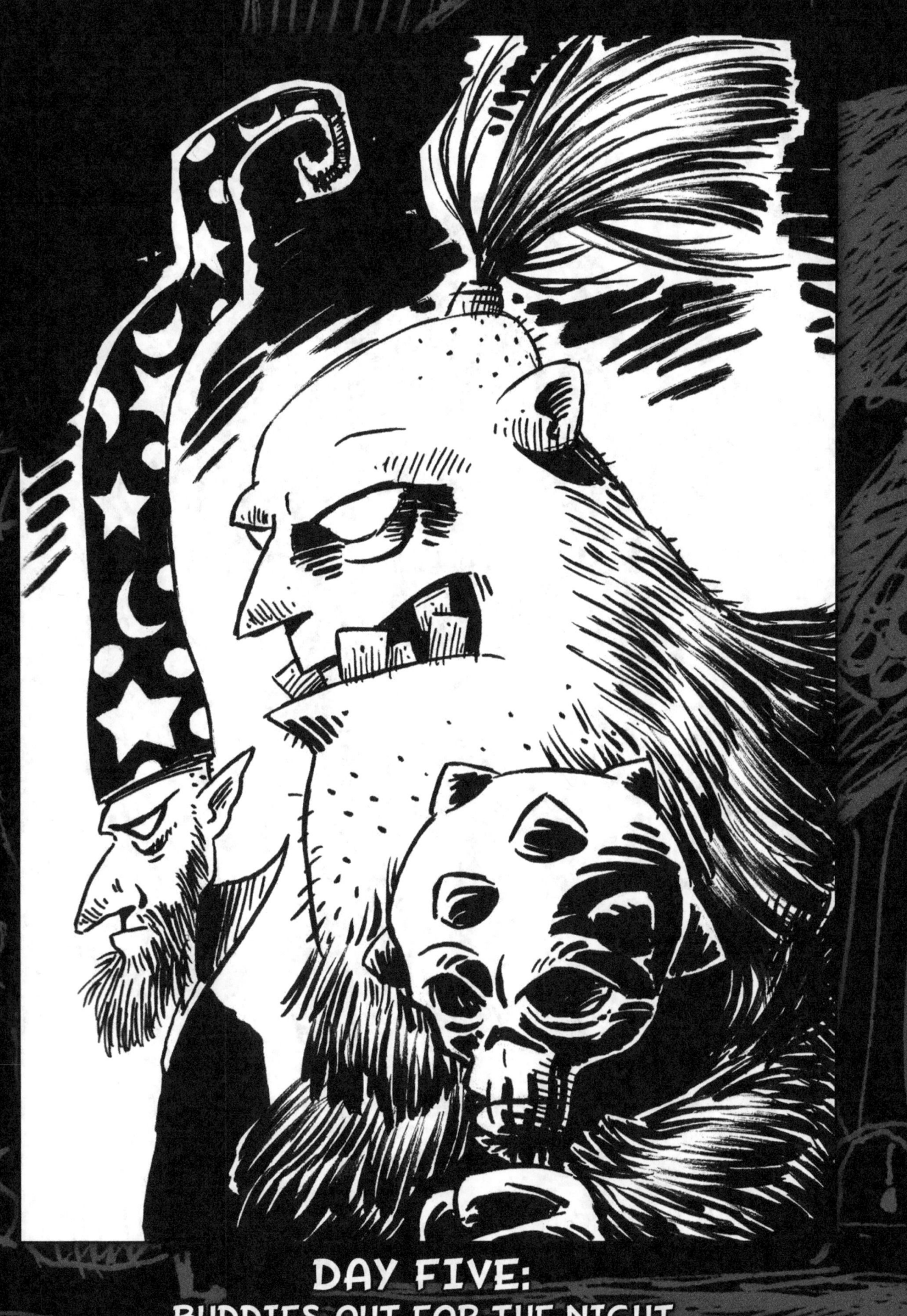

DAY FIVE:
BUDDIES OUT FOR THE NIGHT

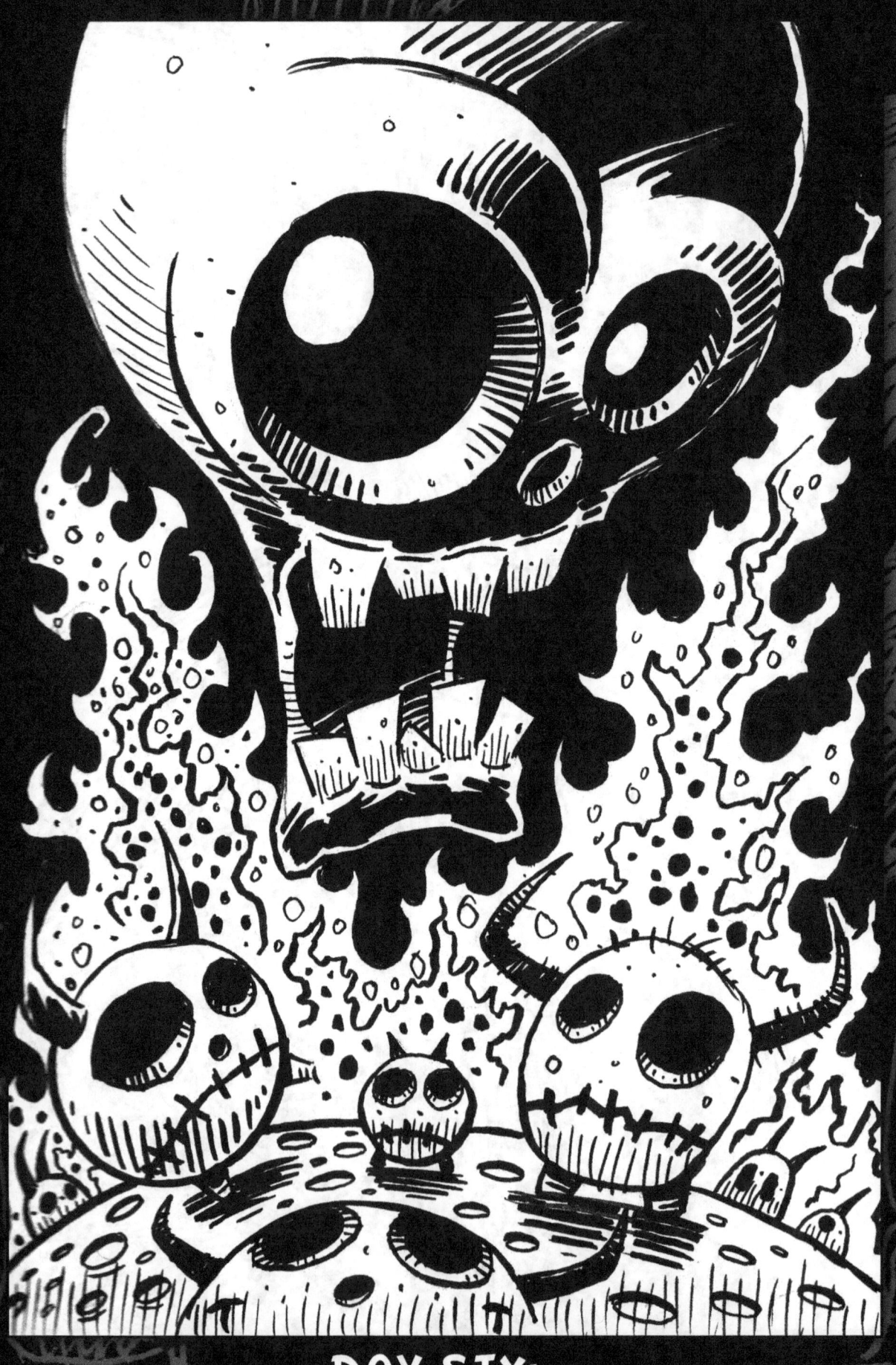

DAY SIX:
SKULL PLANET LORD

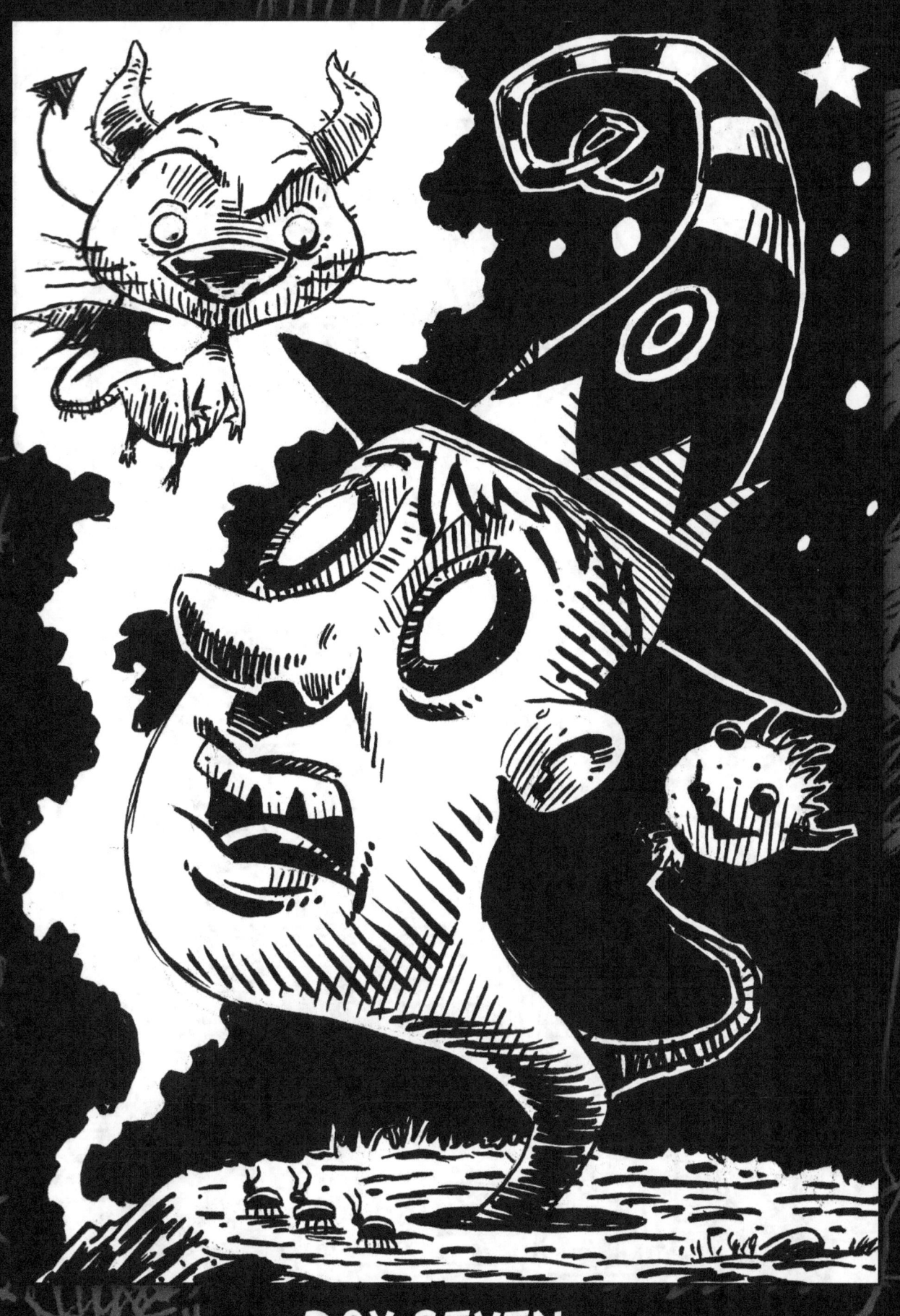

DAY SEVEN:
WORM NIGHT DREAMS

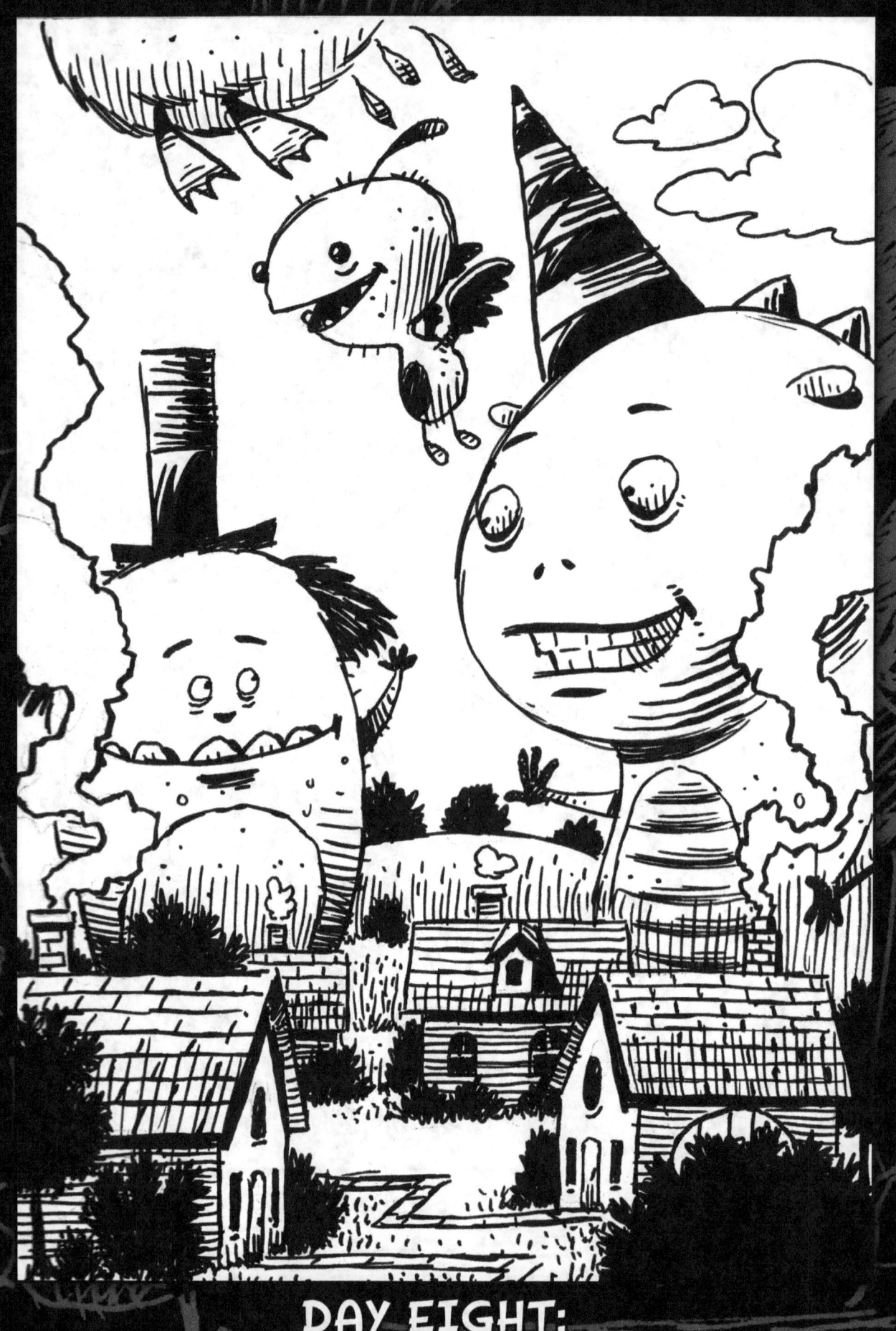

DAY EIGHT:
FRIENDLY NEIGHBORS

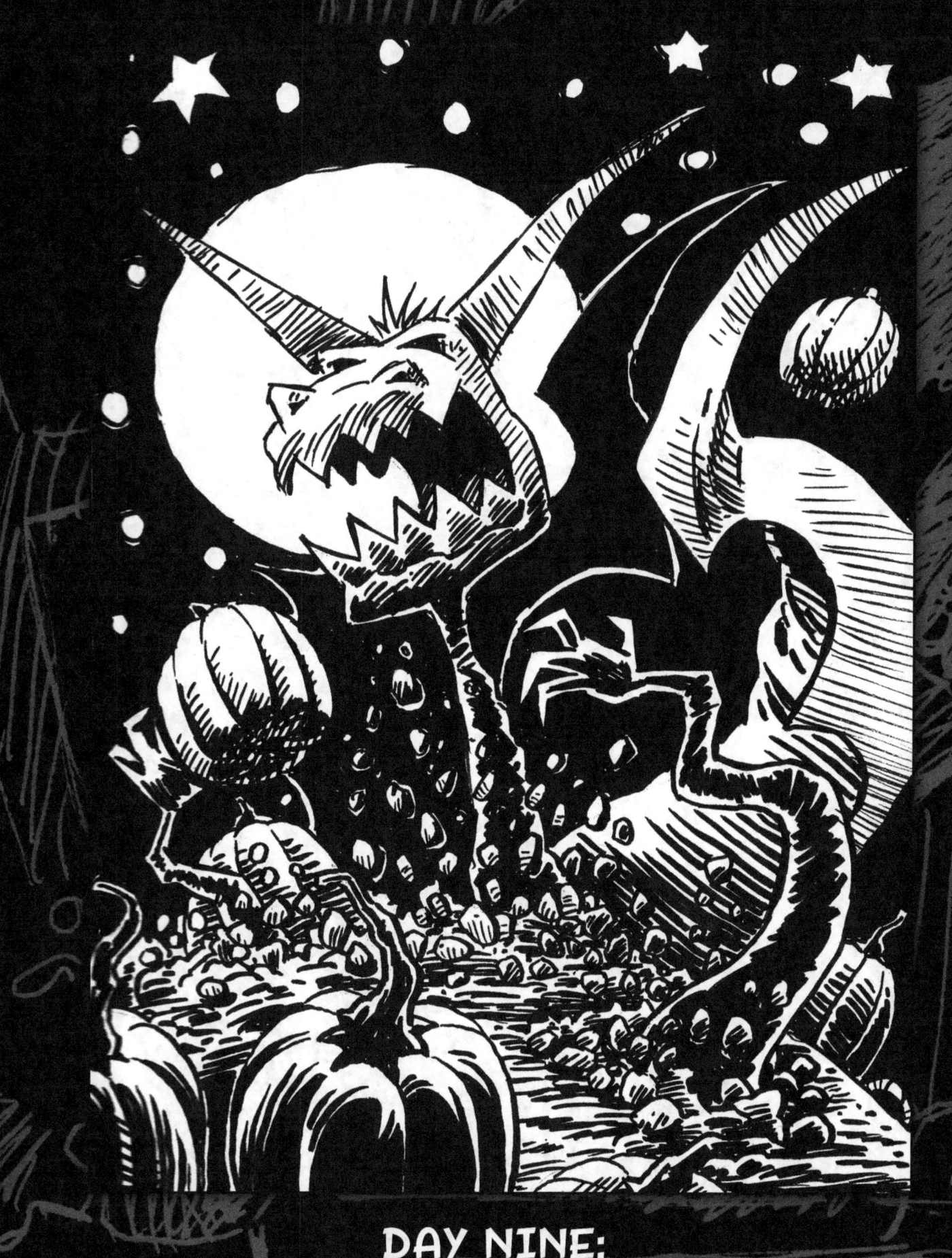

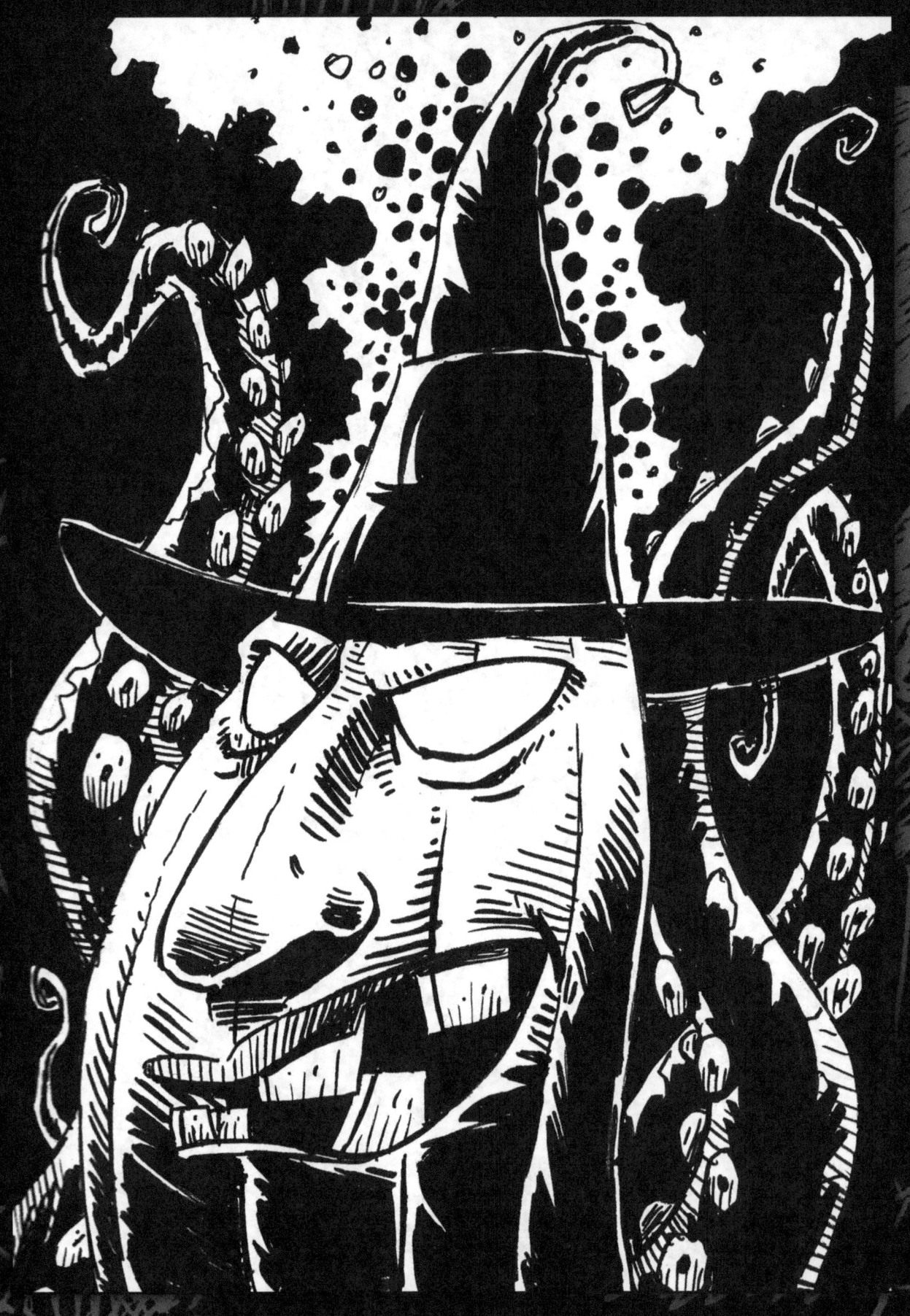

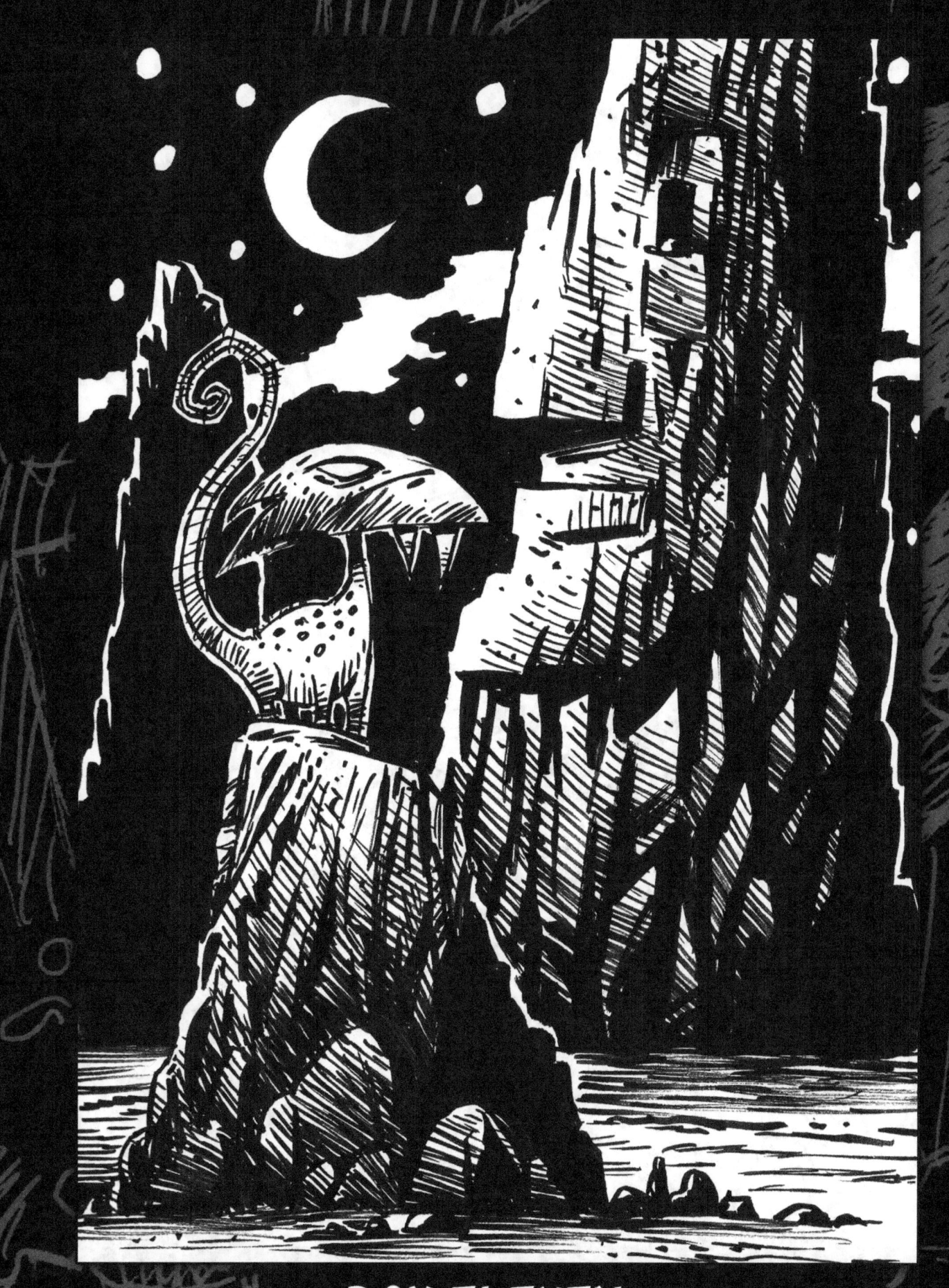

DAY ELEVEN:
MY FRIEND THE SENTINAL

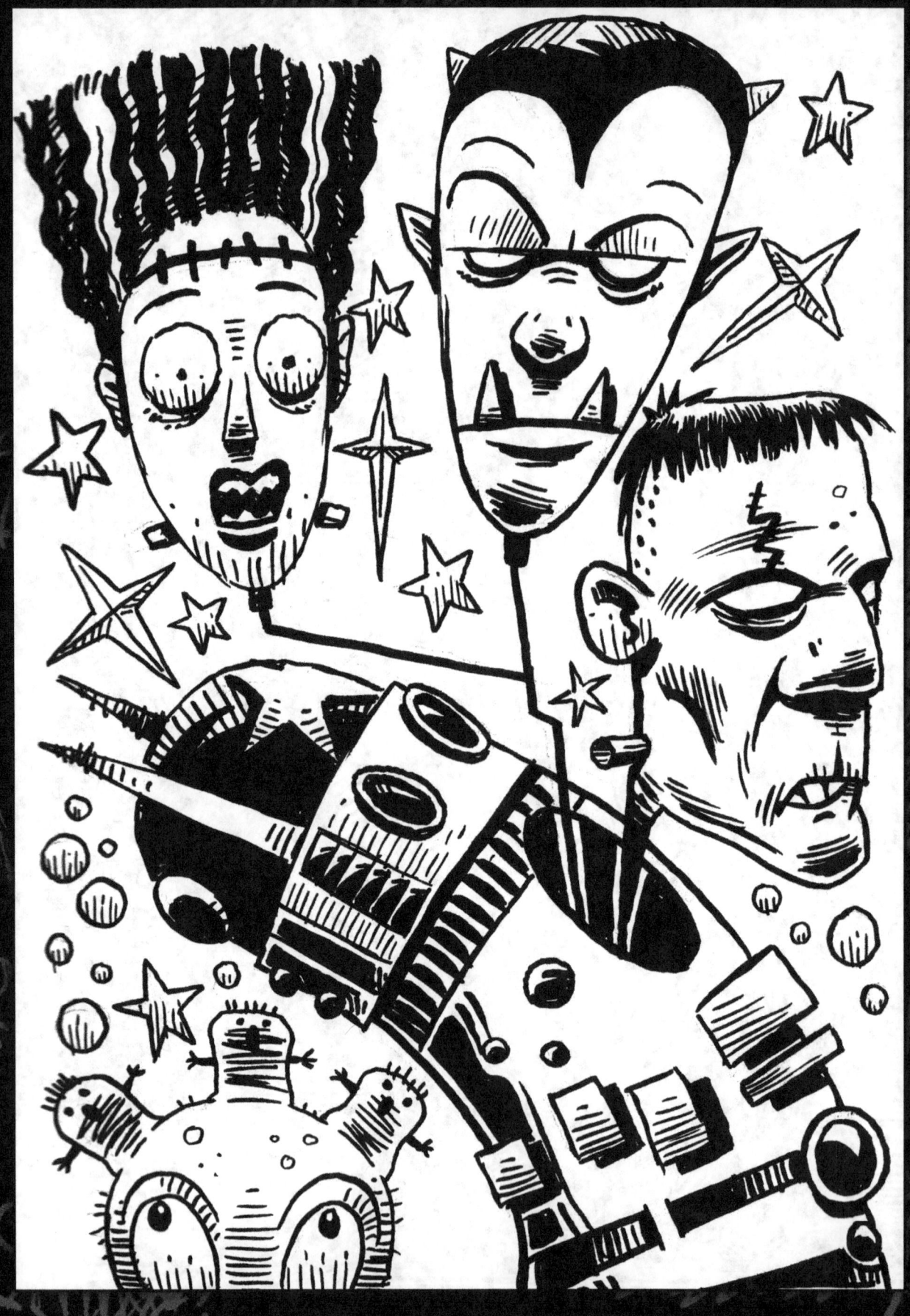

DAY TWELVE:
MONSTERS OUT OF MOUTH

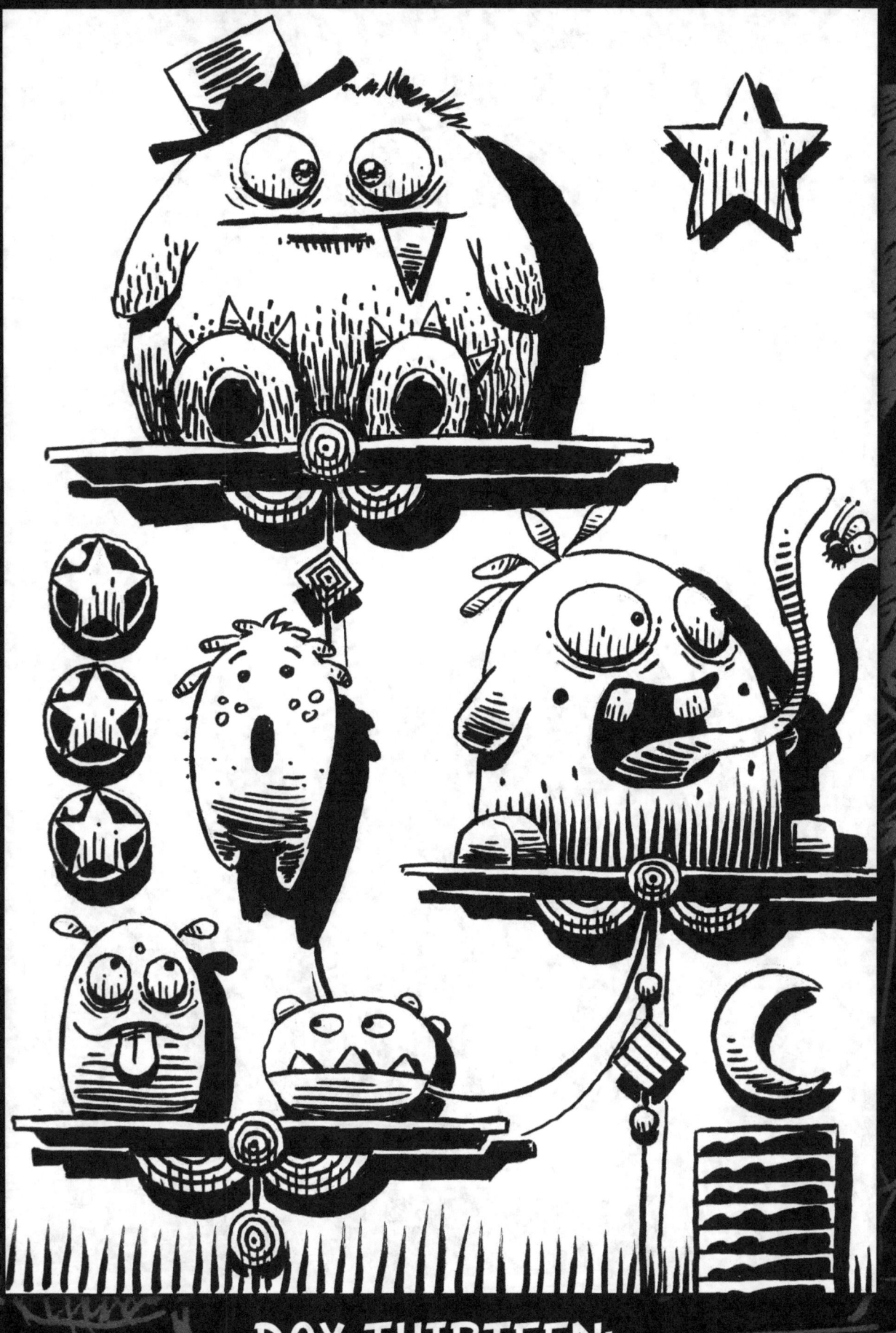

DAY THIRTEEN:
MONSTERS SHELF GAME

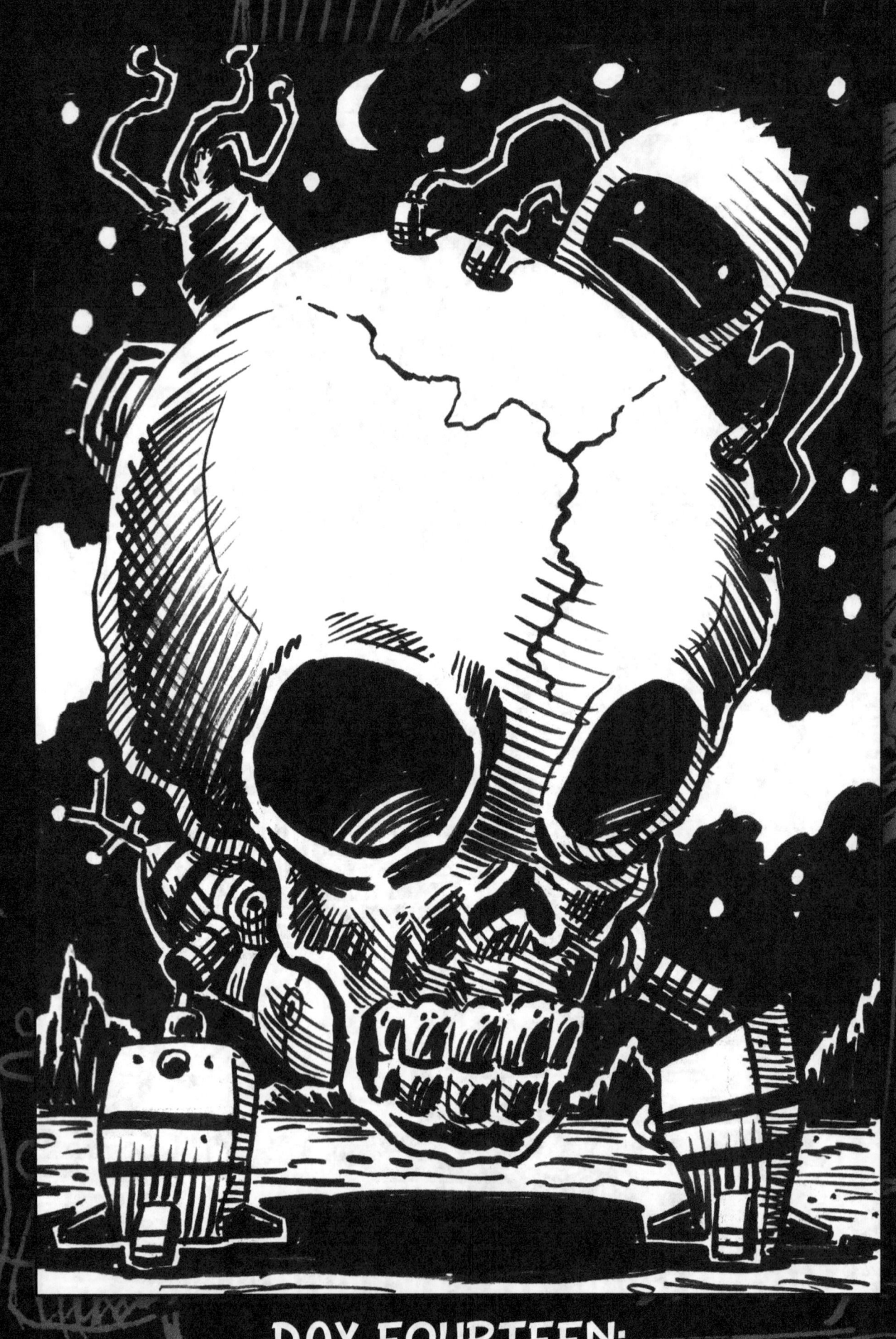

DAY FOURTEEN:
SKULL LANDS ON THE MOON

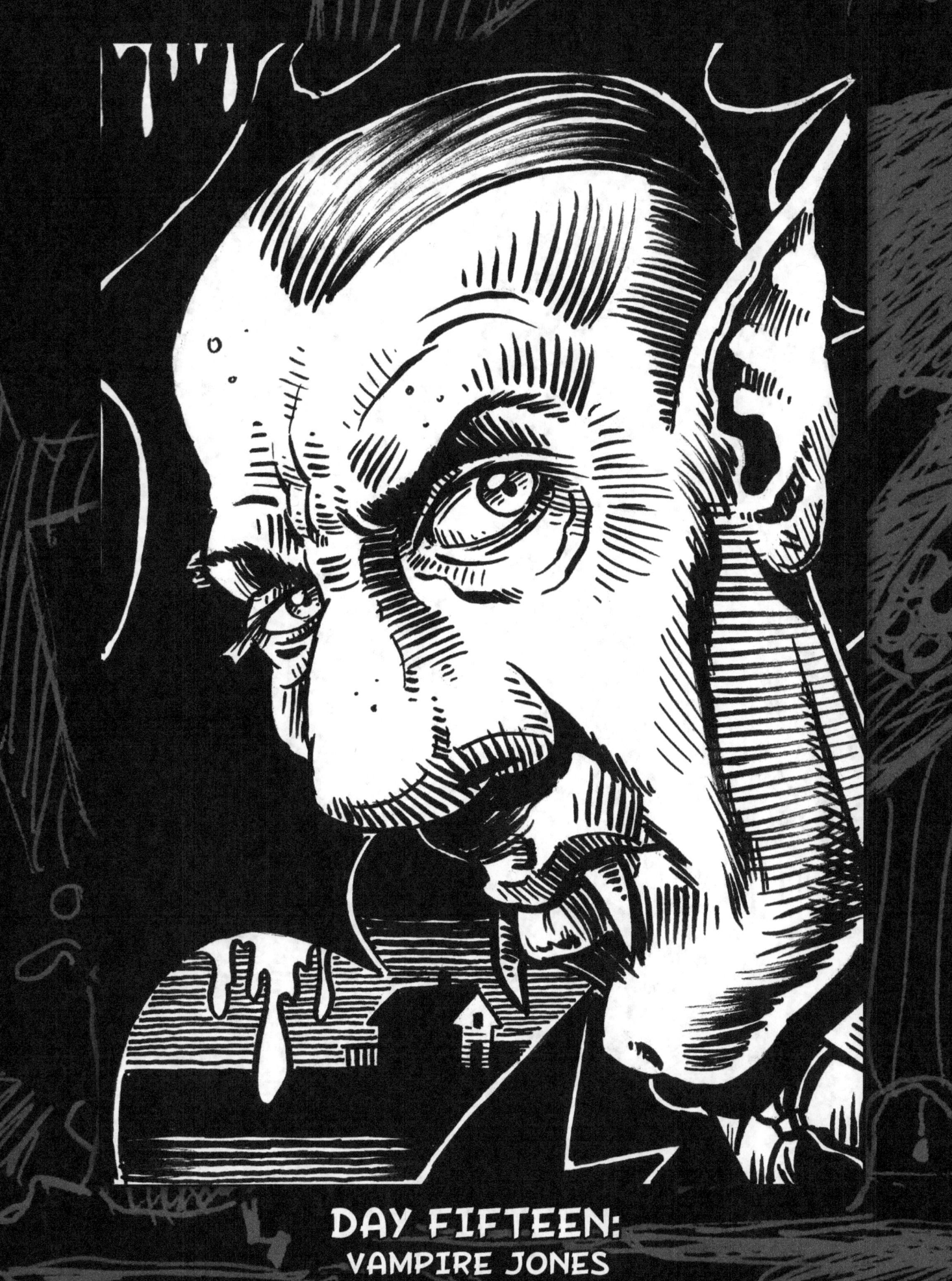

DAY FIFTEEN: VAMPIRE JONES

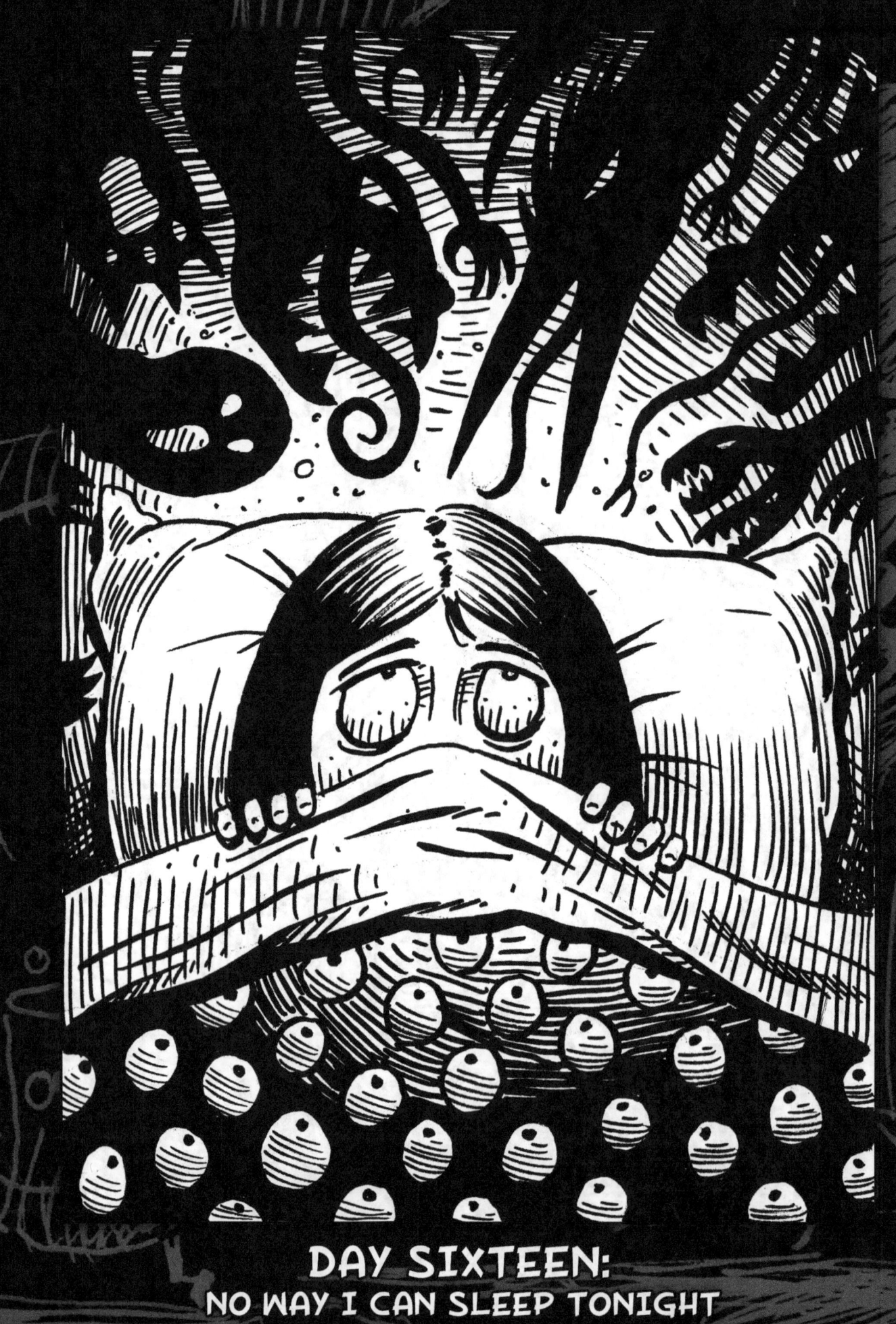

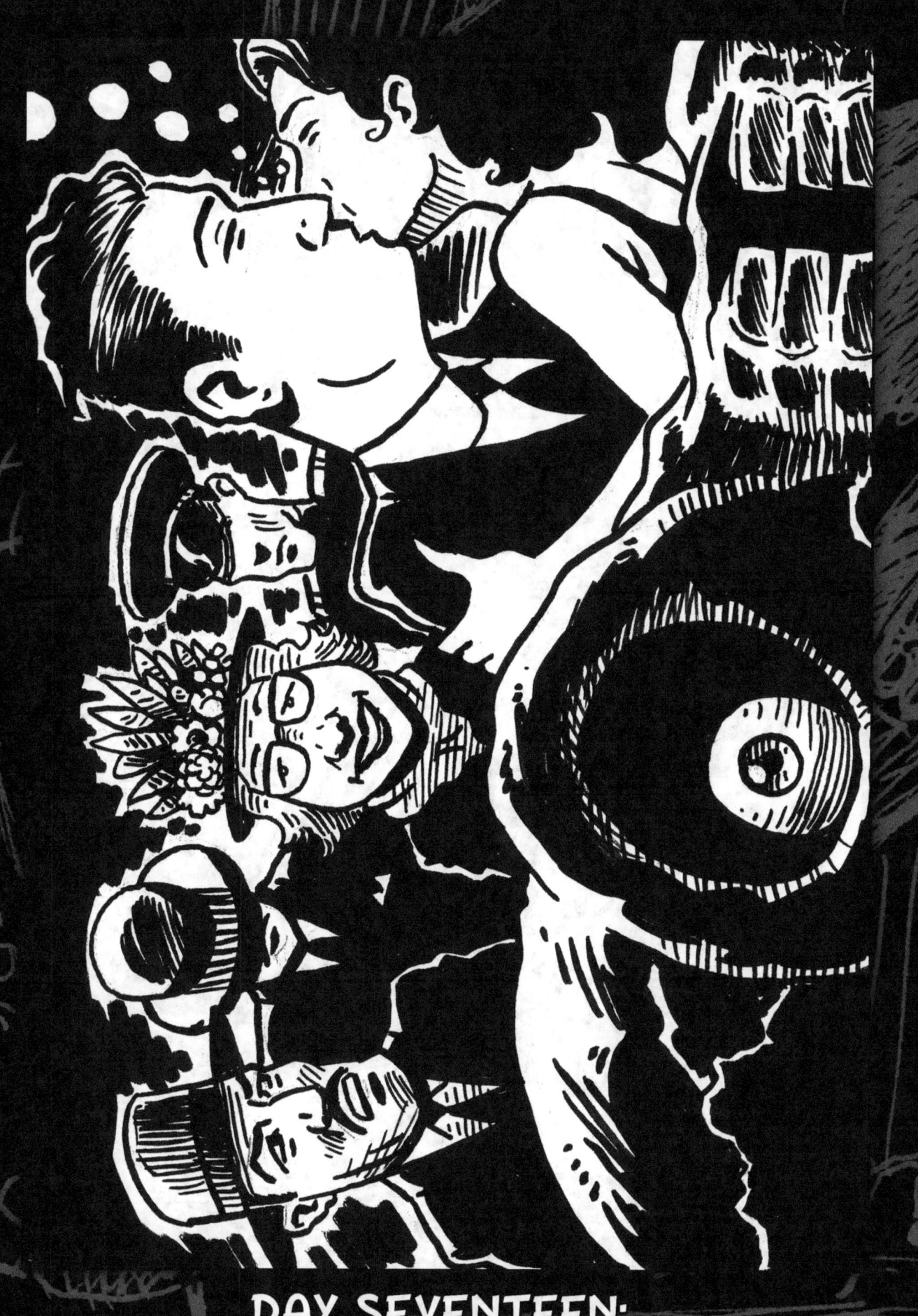

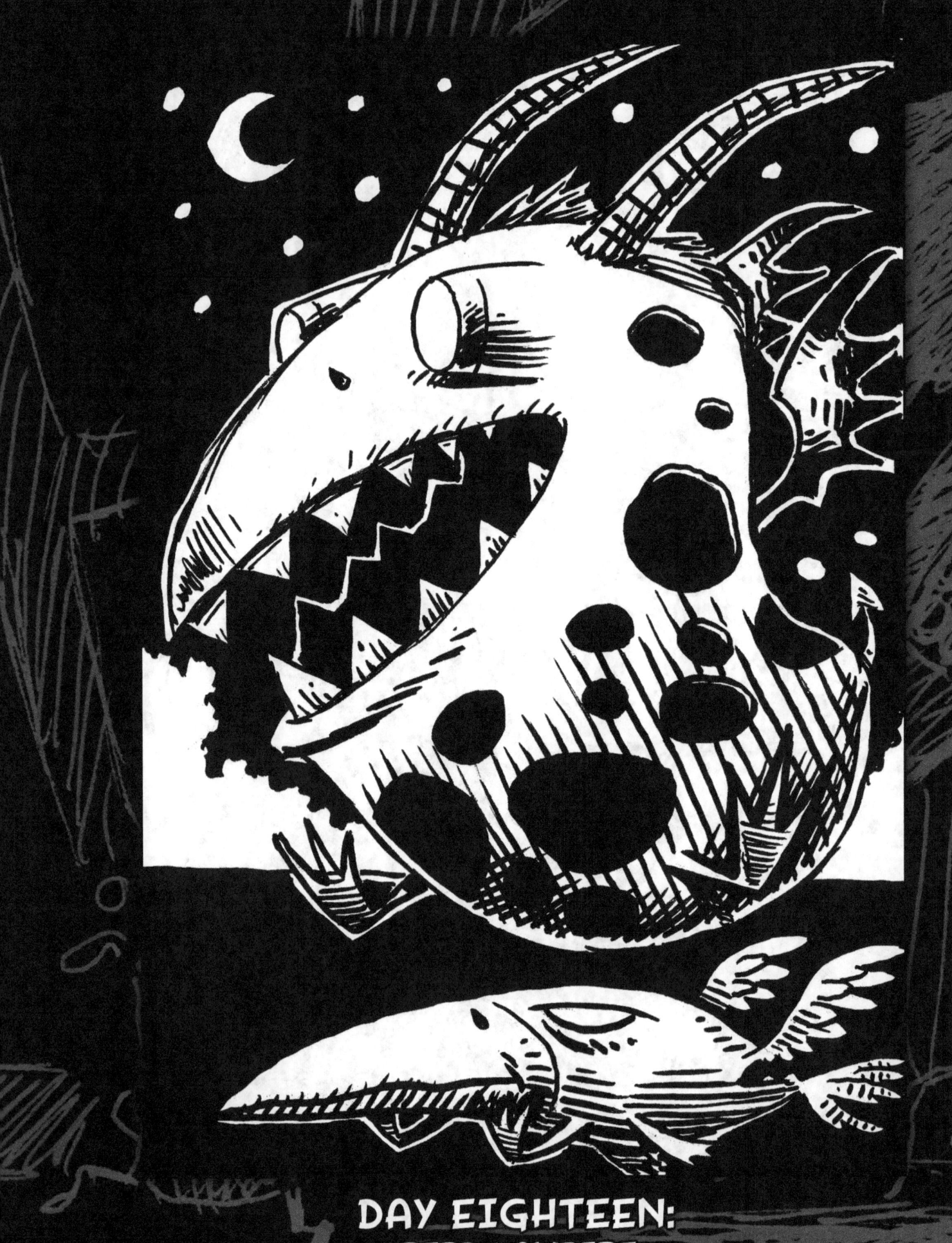

DAY EIGHTEEN:
BIRD VAMPIRE

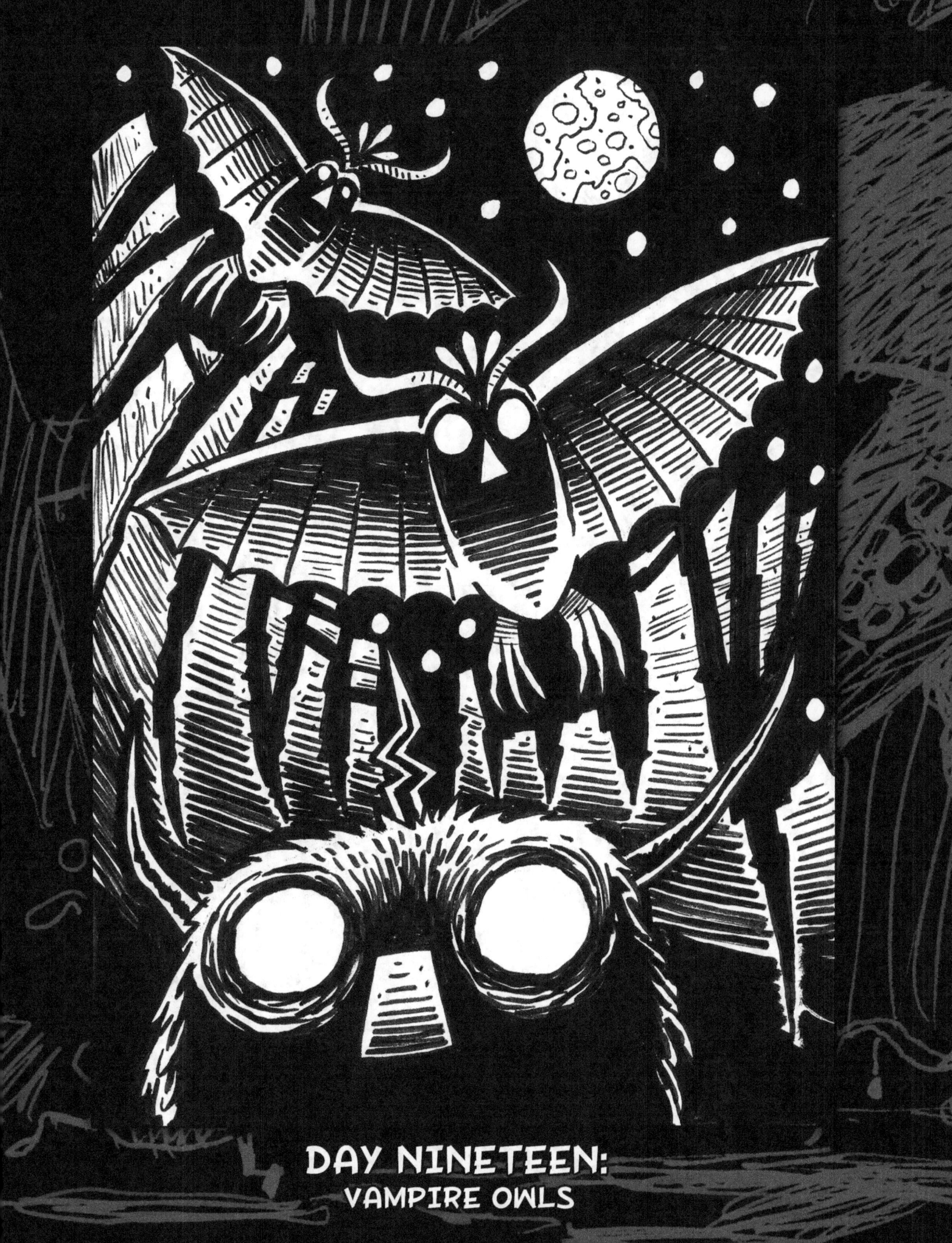

DAY NINETEEN:
VAMPIRE OWLS

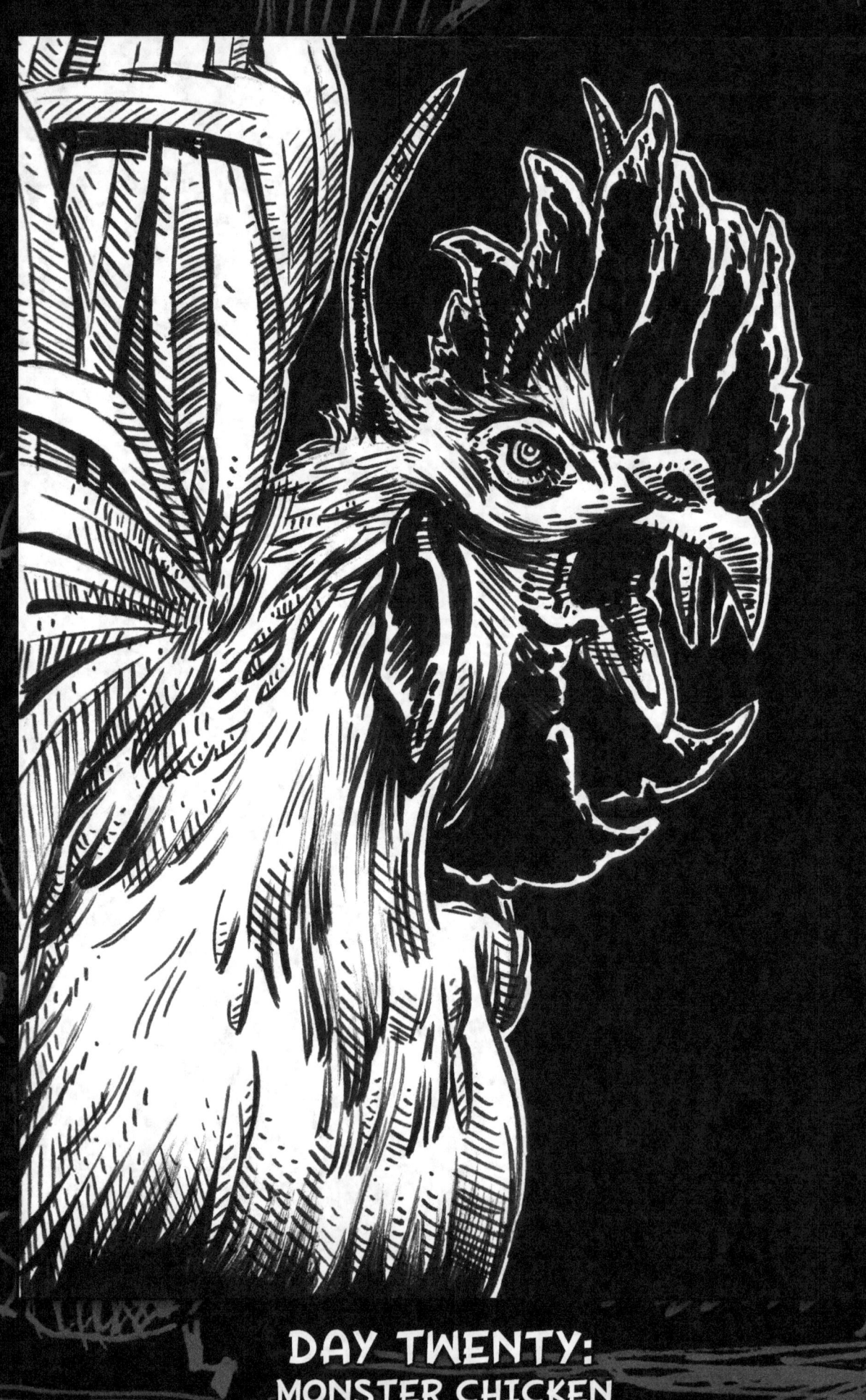

DAY TWENTY:
MONSTER CHICKEN

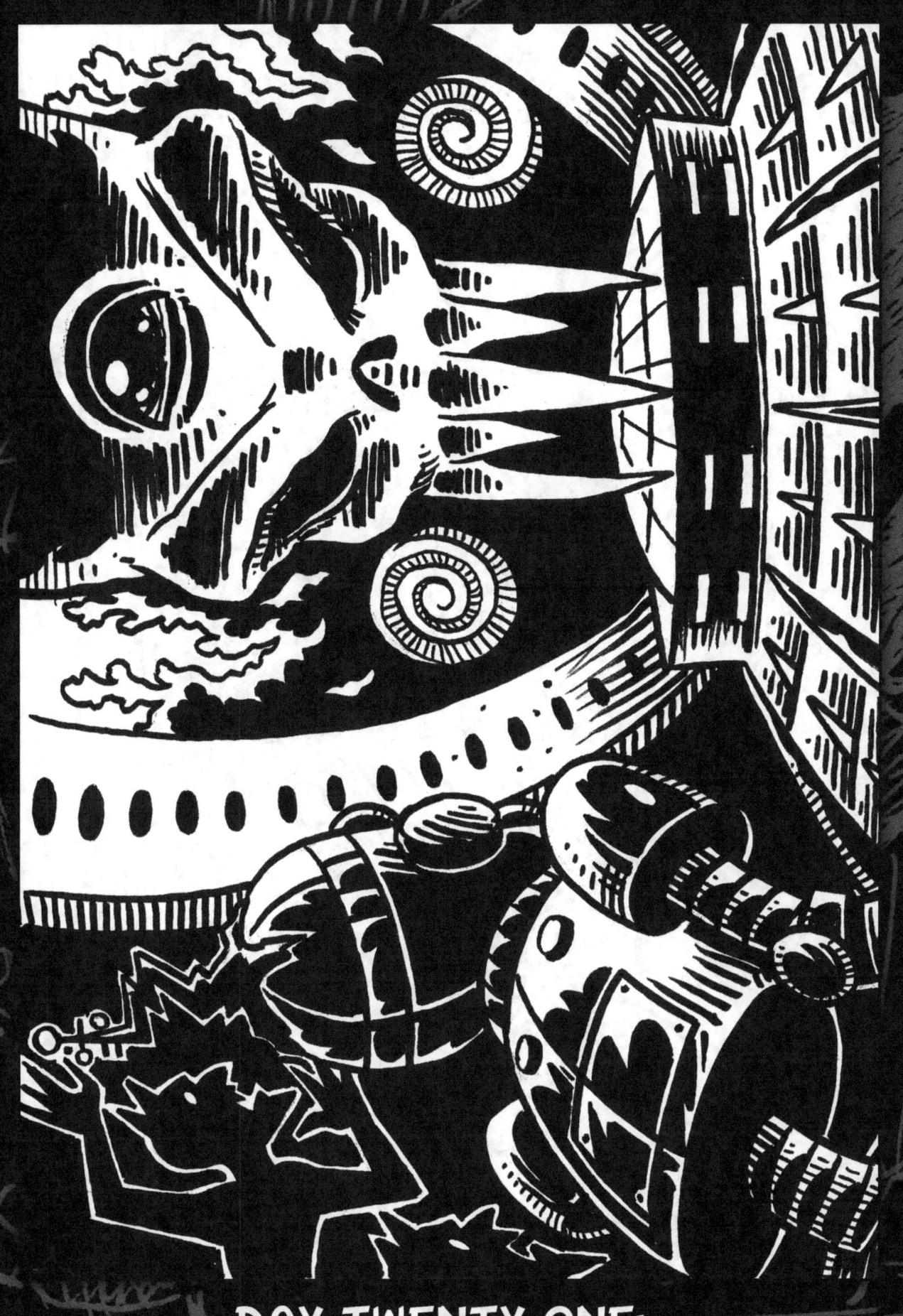

DAY TWENTY ONE:
THE SKULL COMMANDS

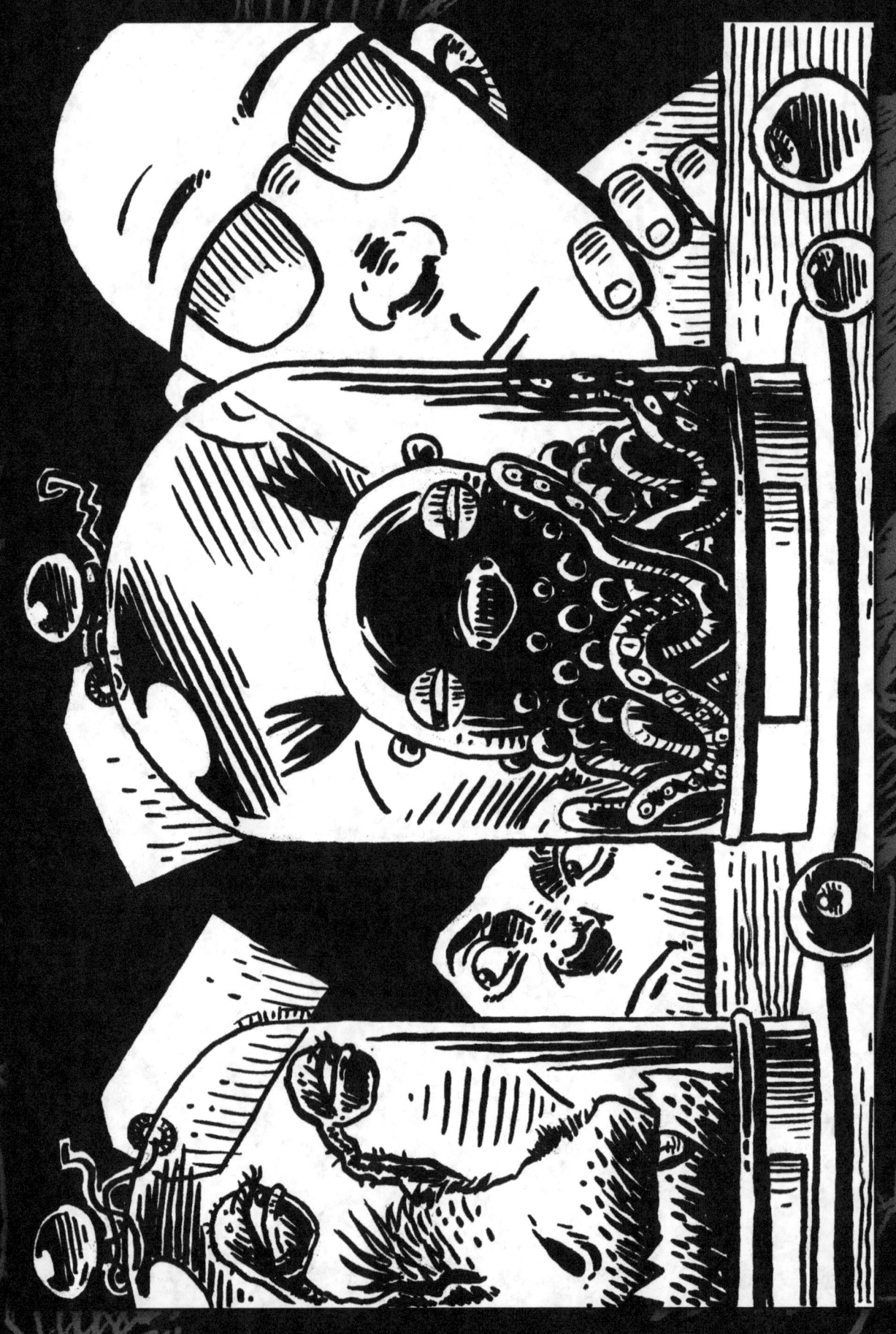

DAY TWENTY TWO:
DOCTOR'S SPECIMENS

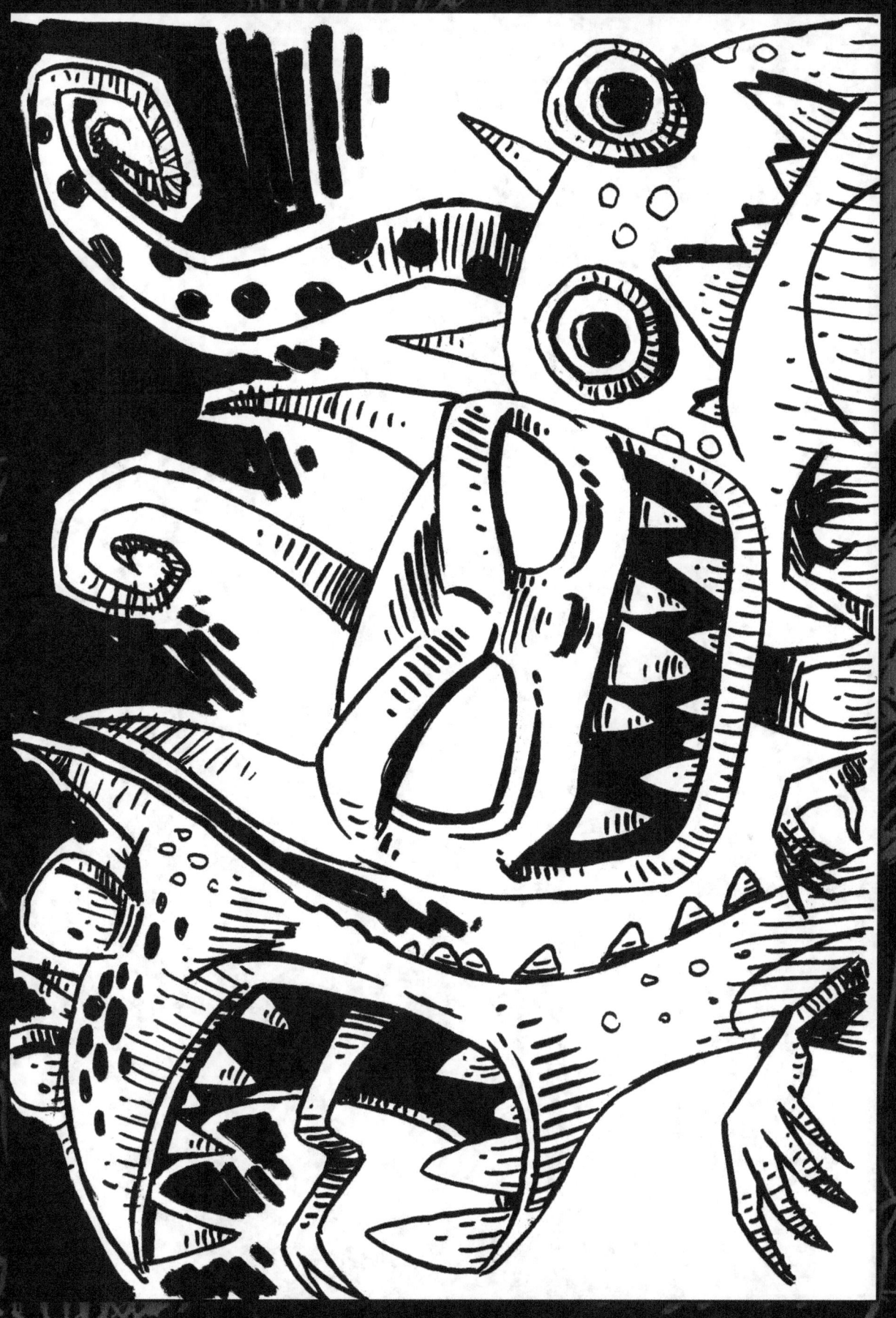

DAY TWENTY THREE:
THREE MONSTROUS FRIENDS

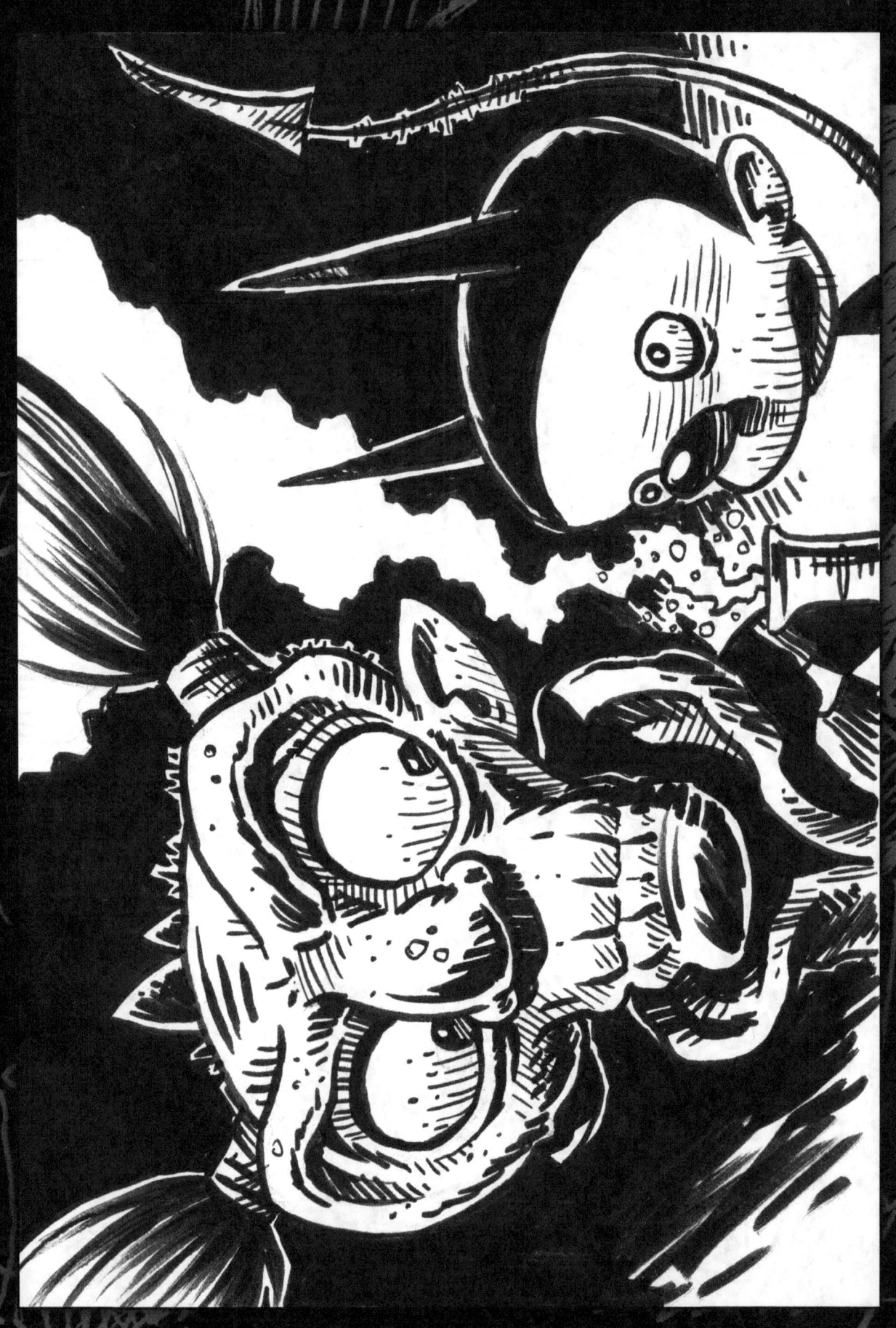

DAY TWENTY FOUR:
THE SCIENCE INTERN

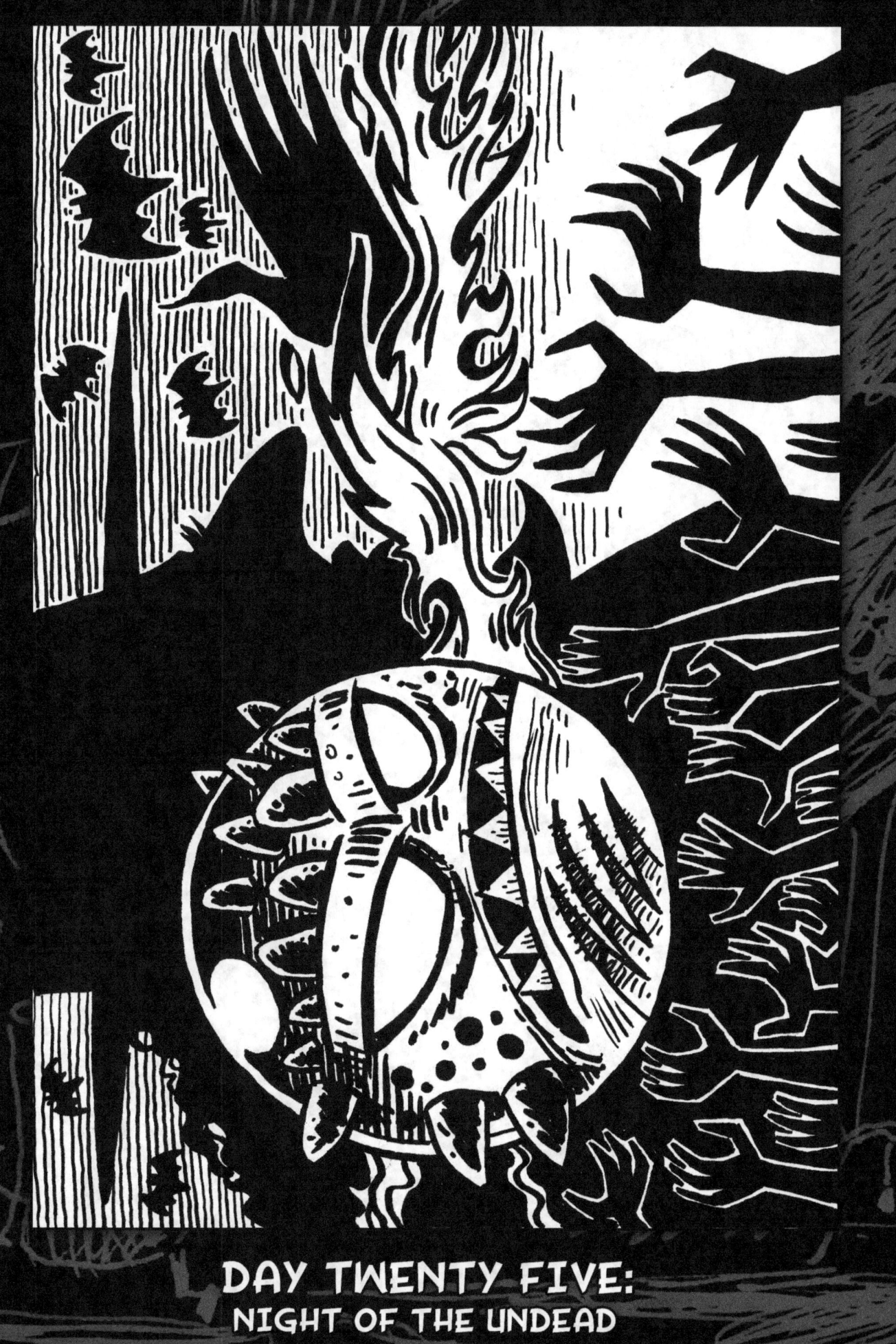

DAY TWENTY FIVE:
NIGHT OF THE UNDEAD

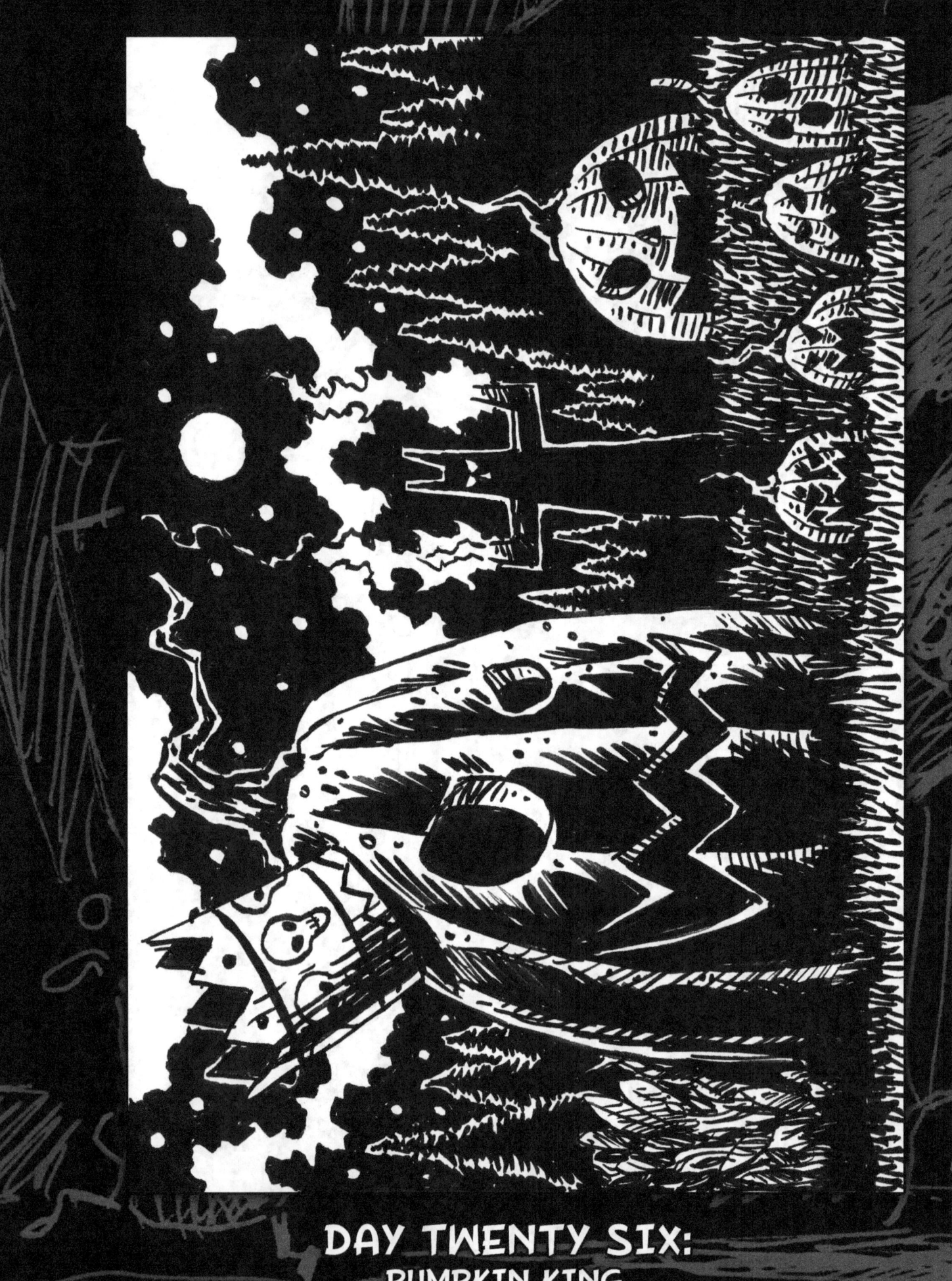

DAY TWENTY SIX:
PUMPKIN KING

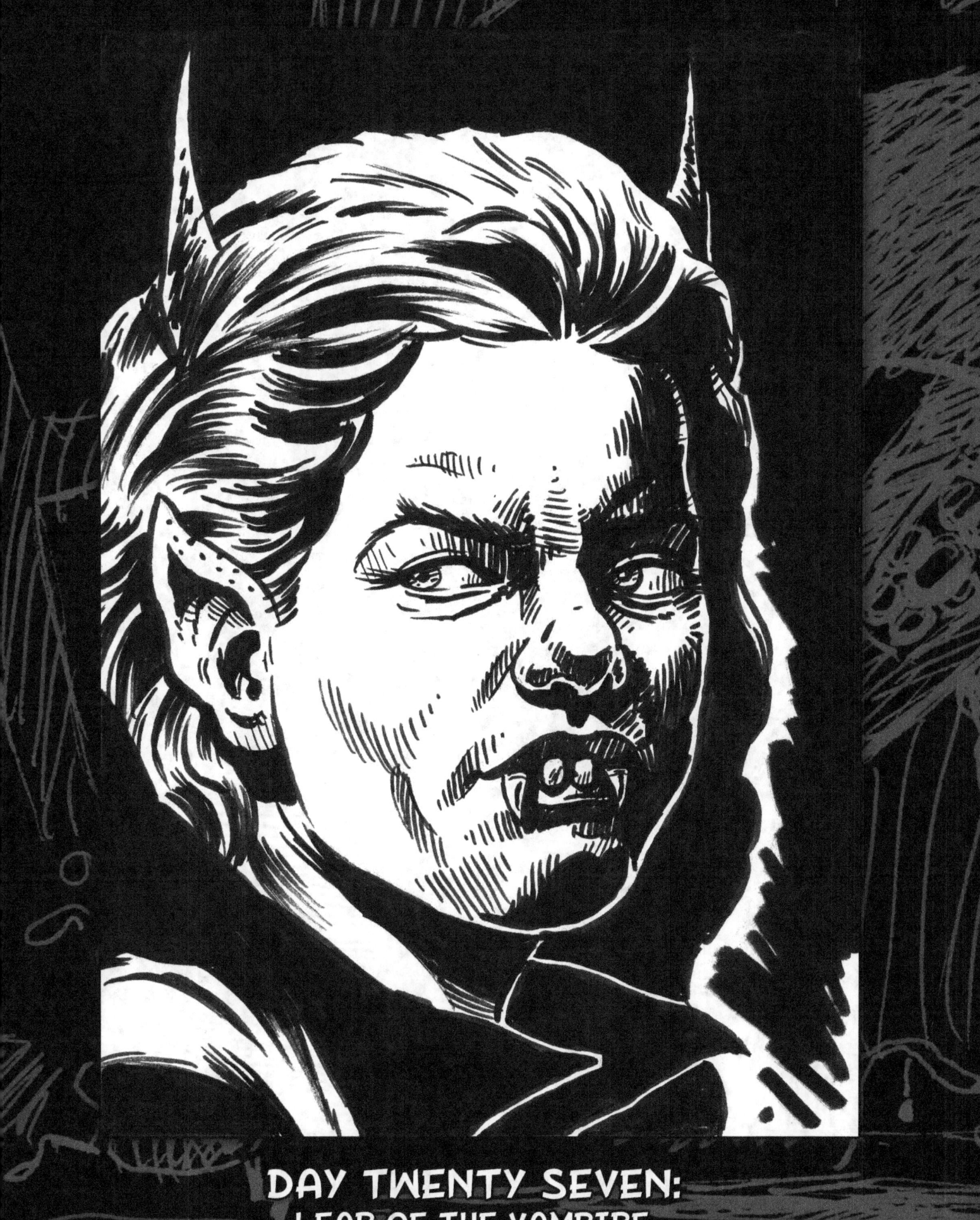

DAY TWENTY SEVEN:
LEAR OF THE VAMPIRE

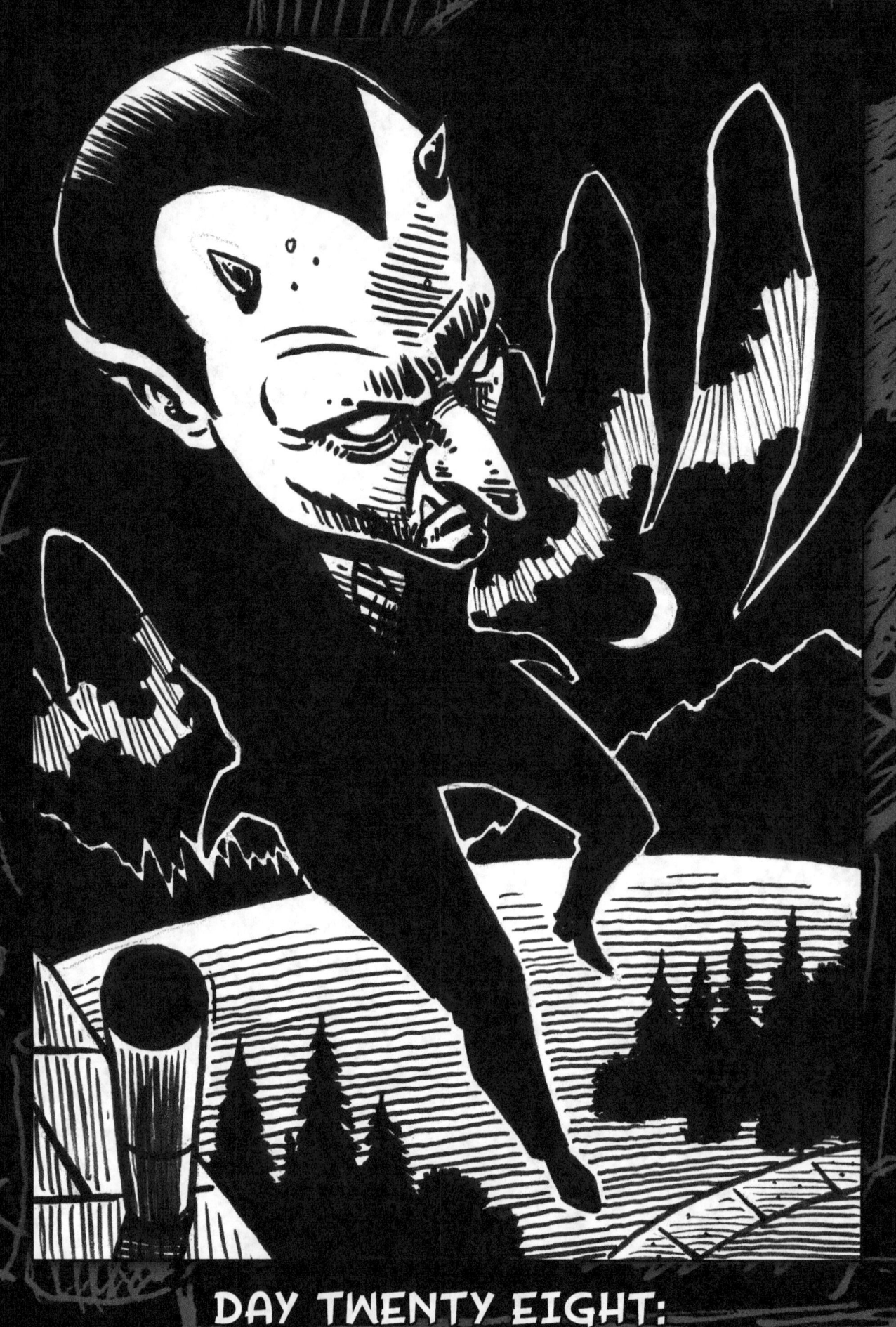

DAY TWENTY EIGHT:
COMING IN FOR A LANDING

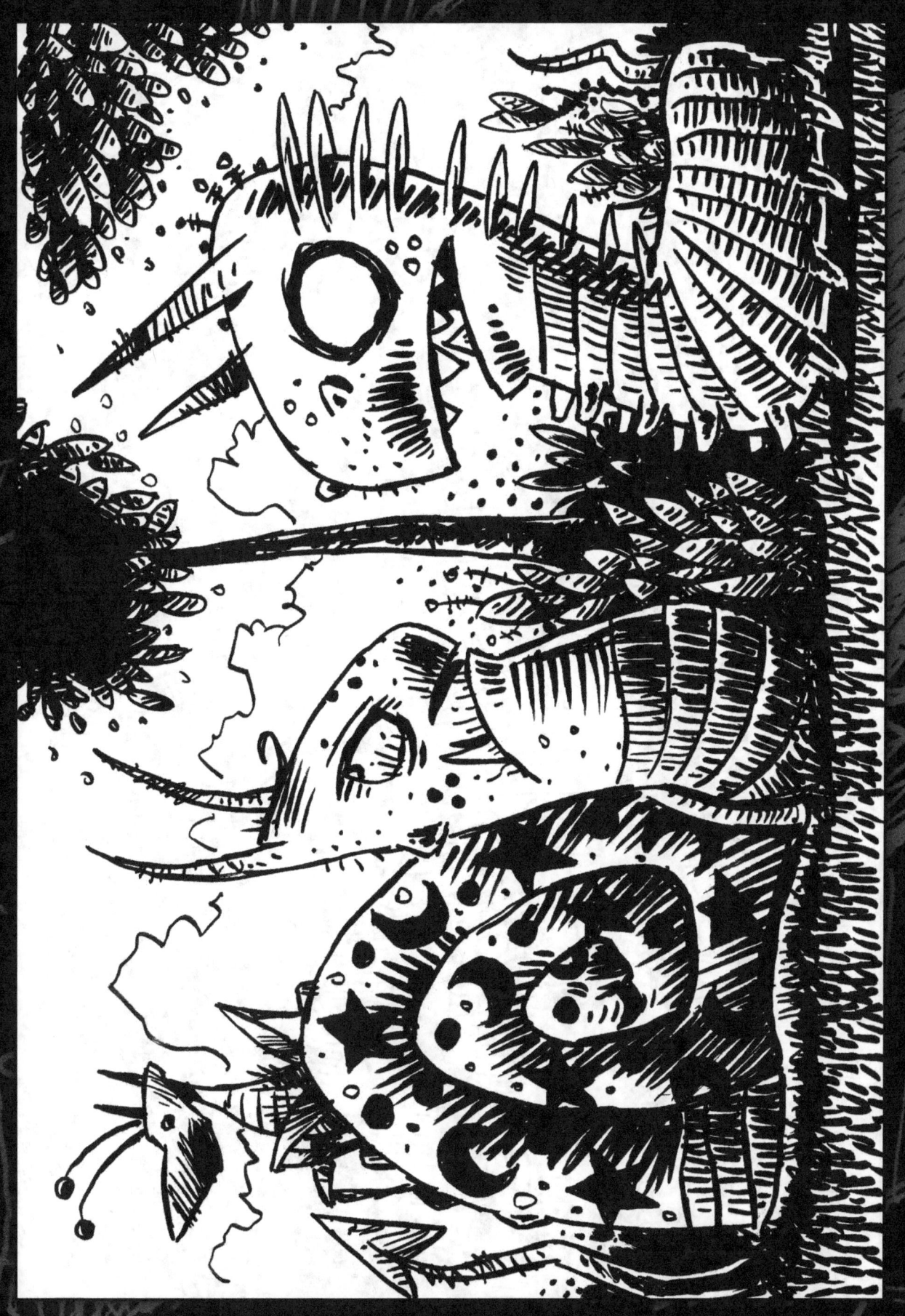

DAY TWENTY NINE:
DEVIL SNAILS

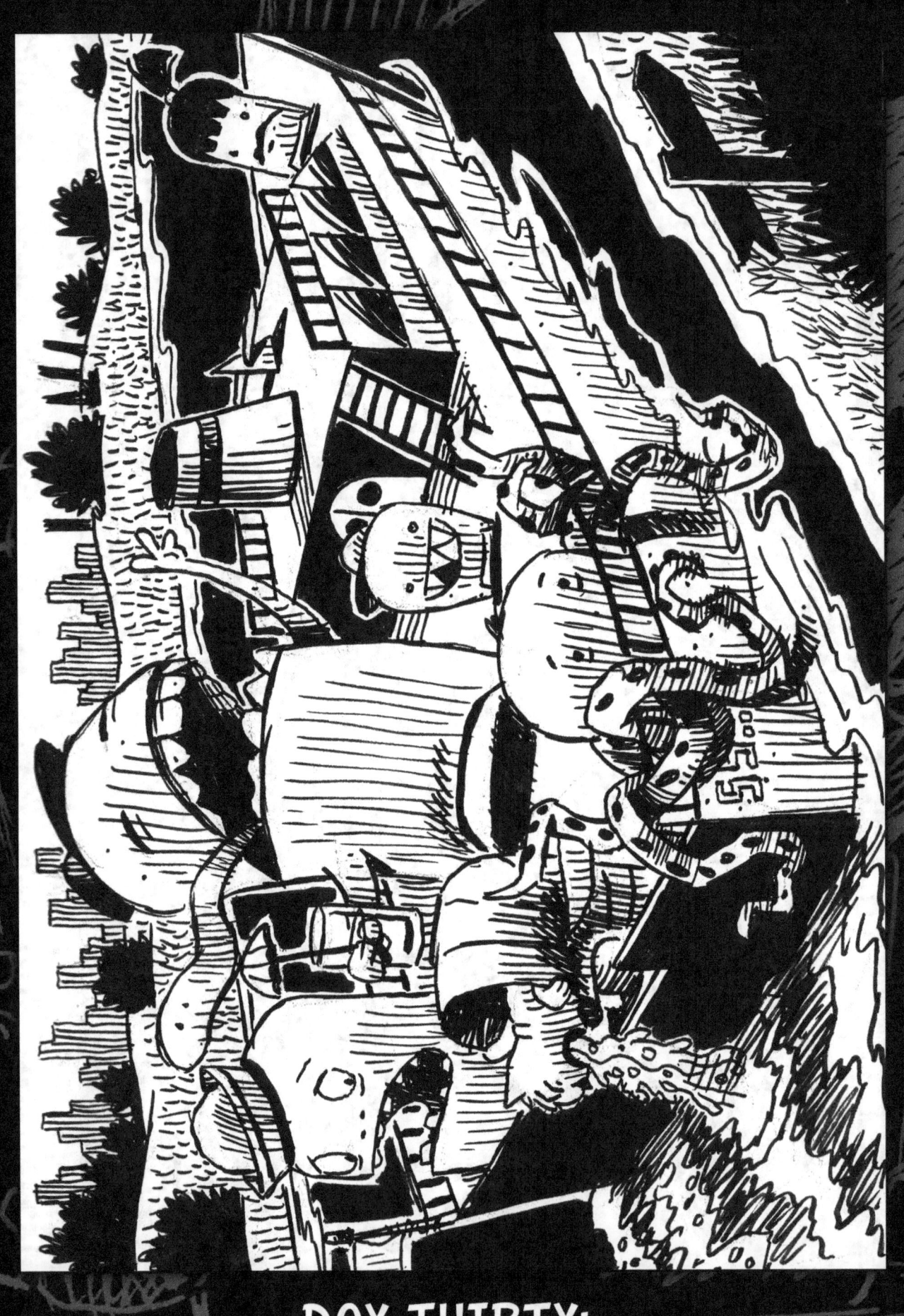

DAY THIRTY:
MONSTER CRUISE

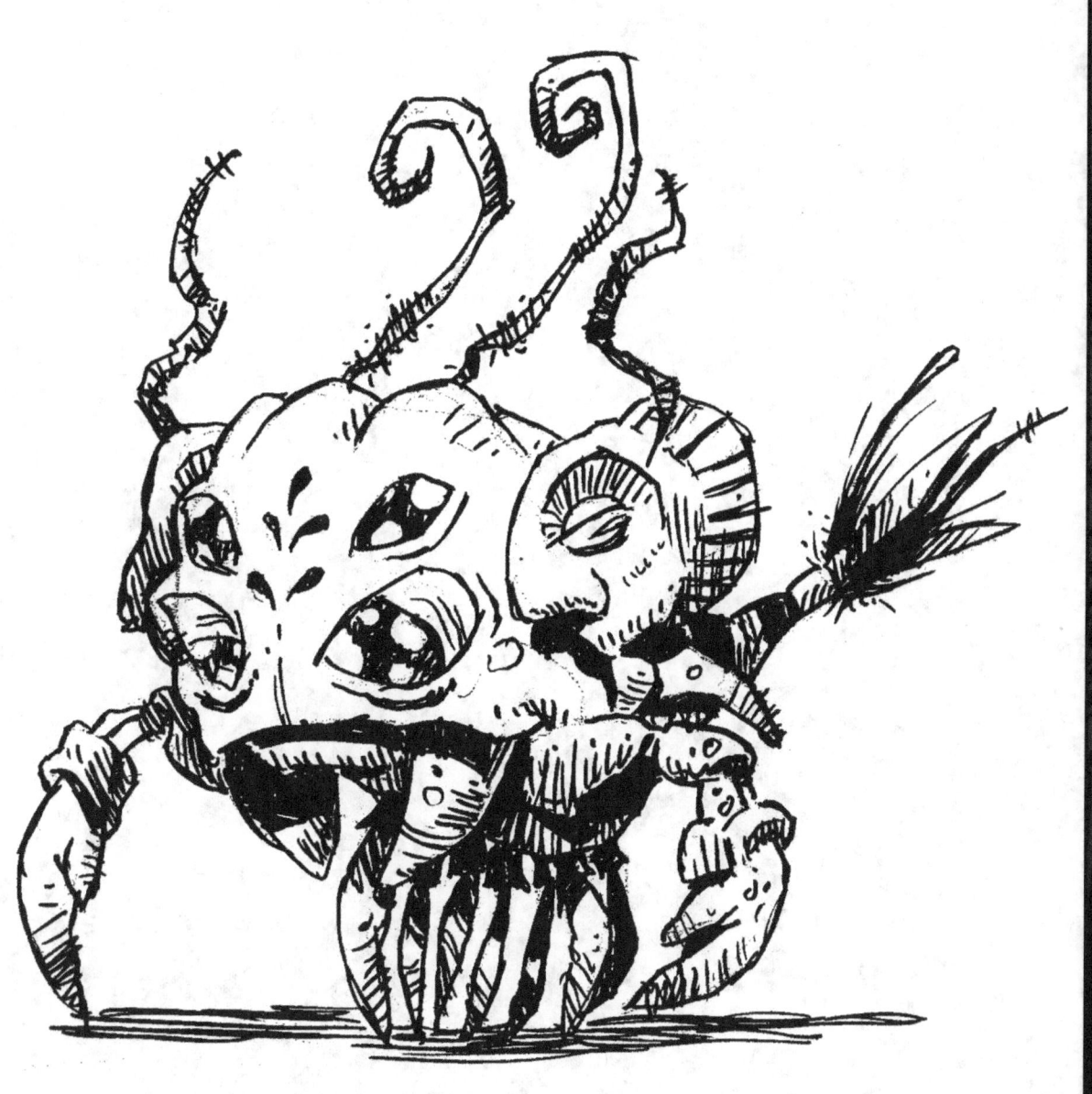

DAY THIRTY ONE:
CUTE LITTLE CREATURE

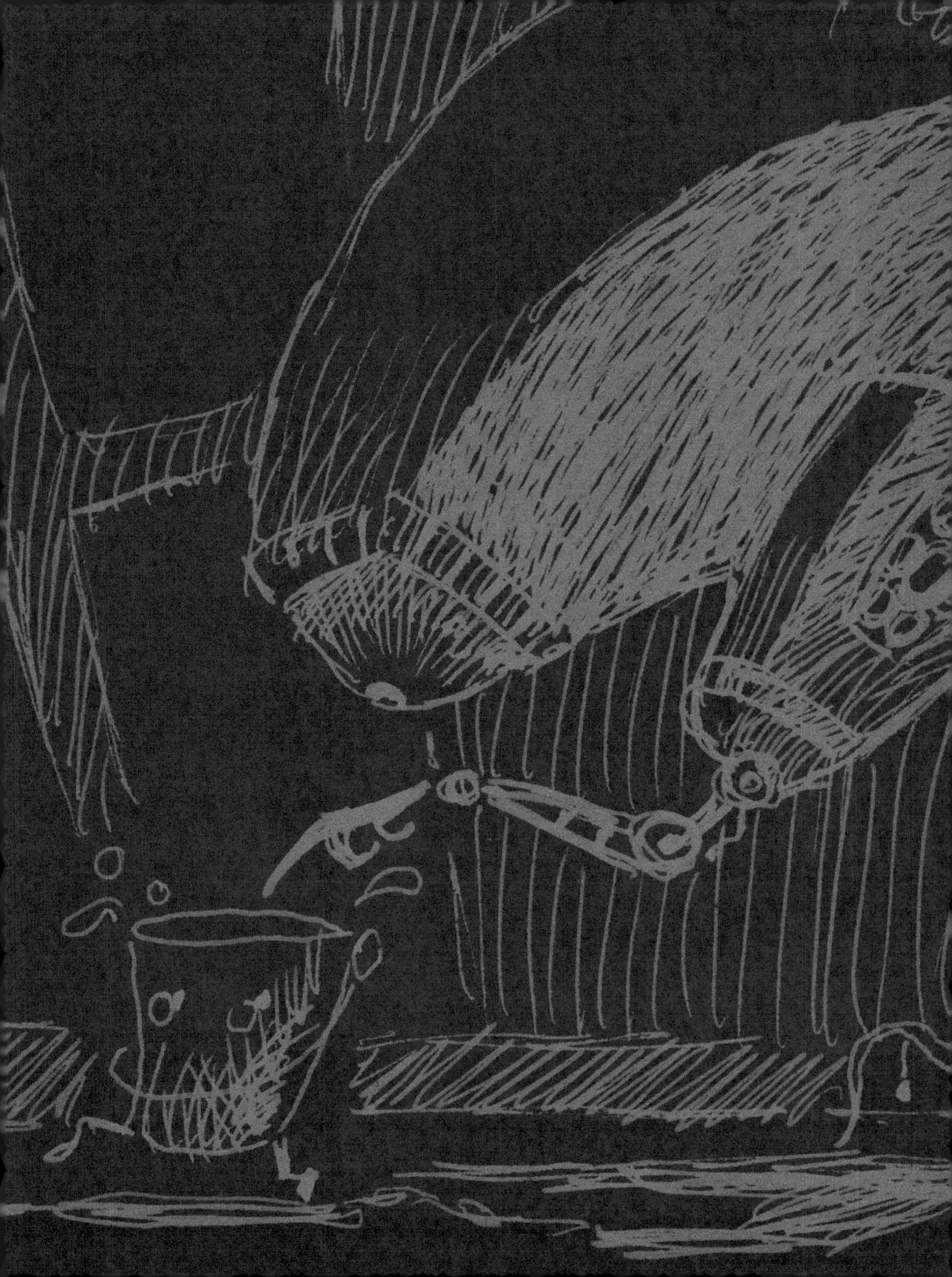

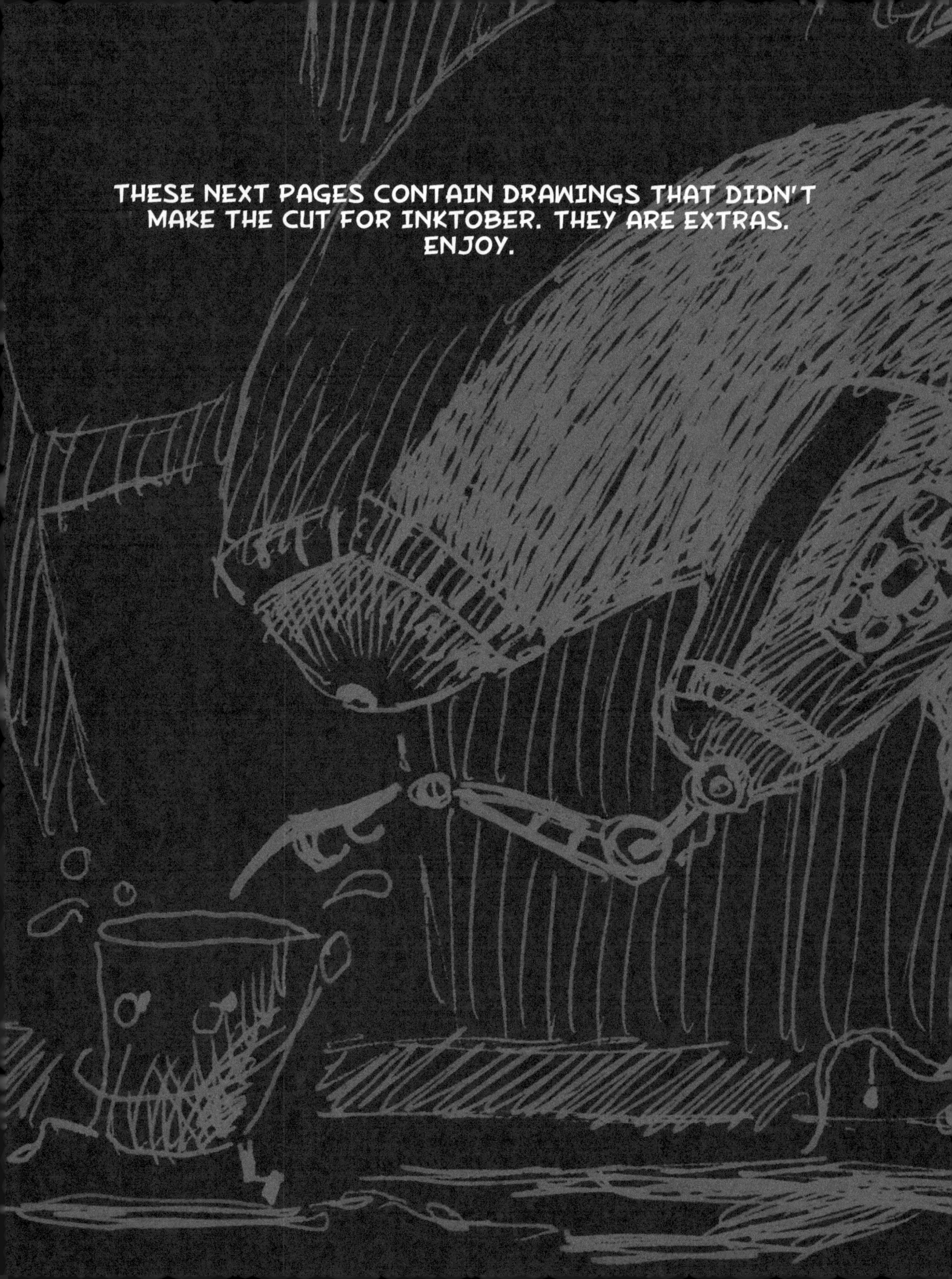

THESE NEXT PAGES CONTAIN DRAWINGS THAT DIDN'T MAKE THE CUT FOR INKTOBER. THEY ARE EXTRAS. ENJOY.

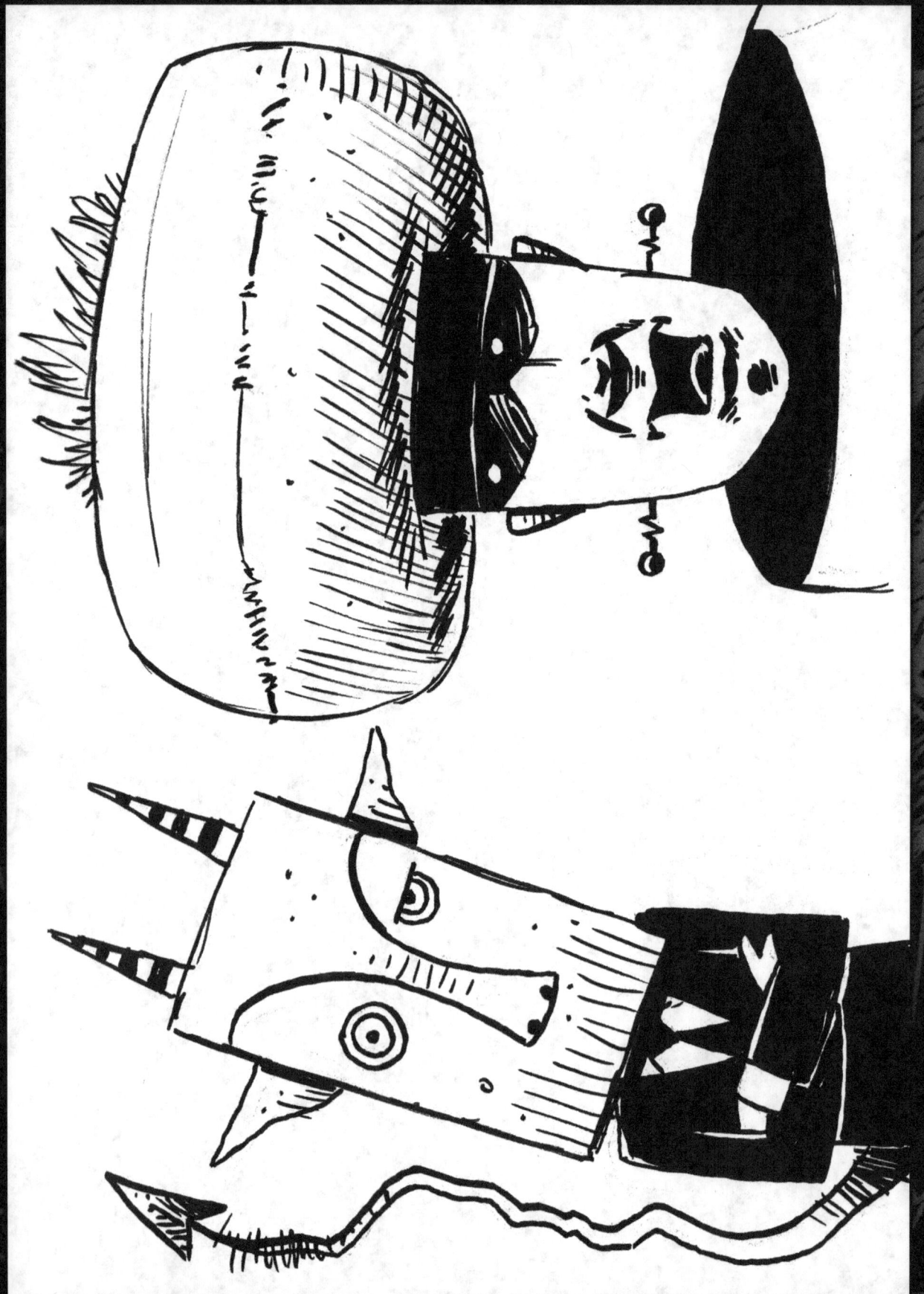

HALLOWEEN COSTUMES

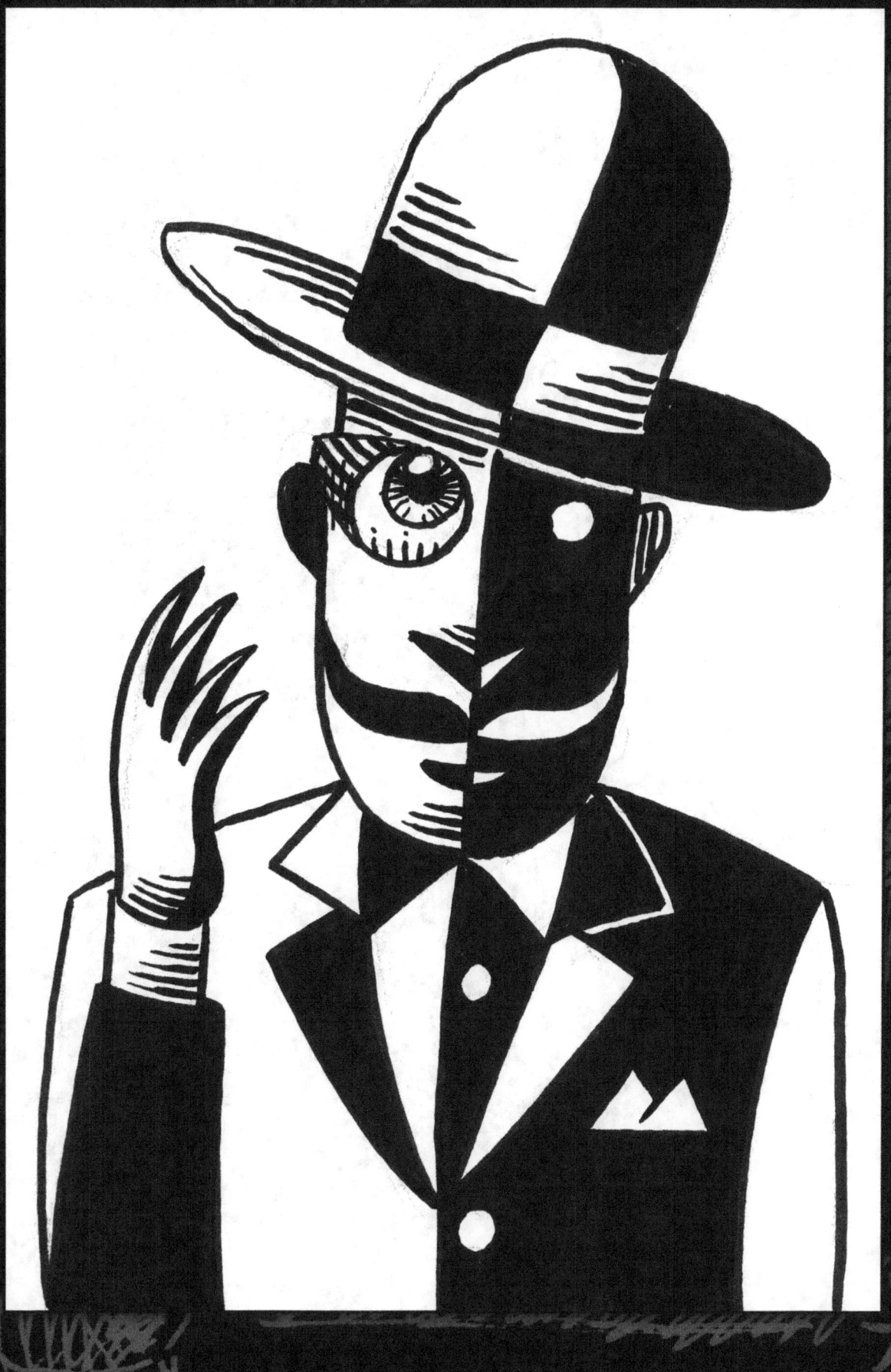

BOTH SIDES OF MIDNIGHT

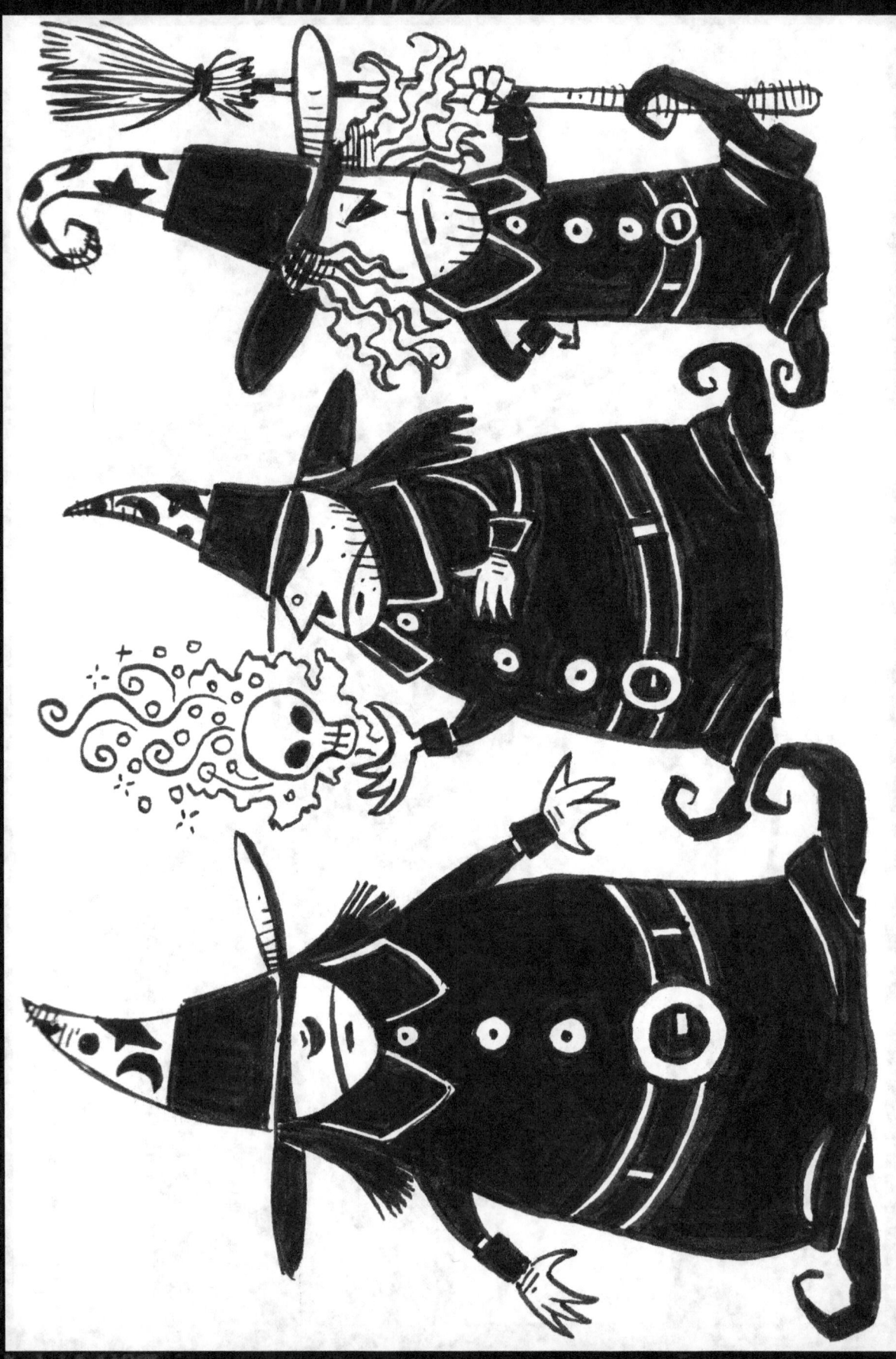

SISTER WITCHES

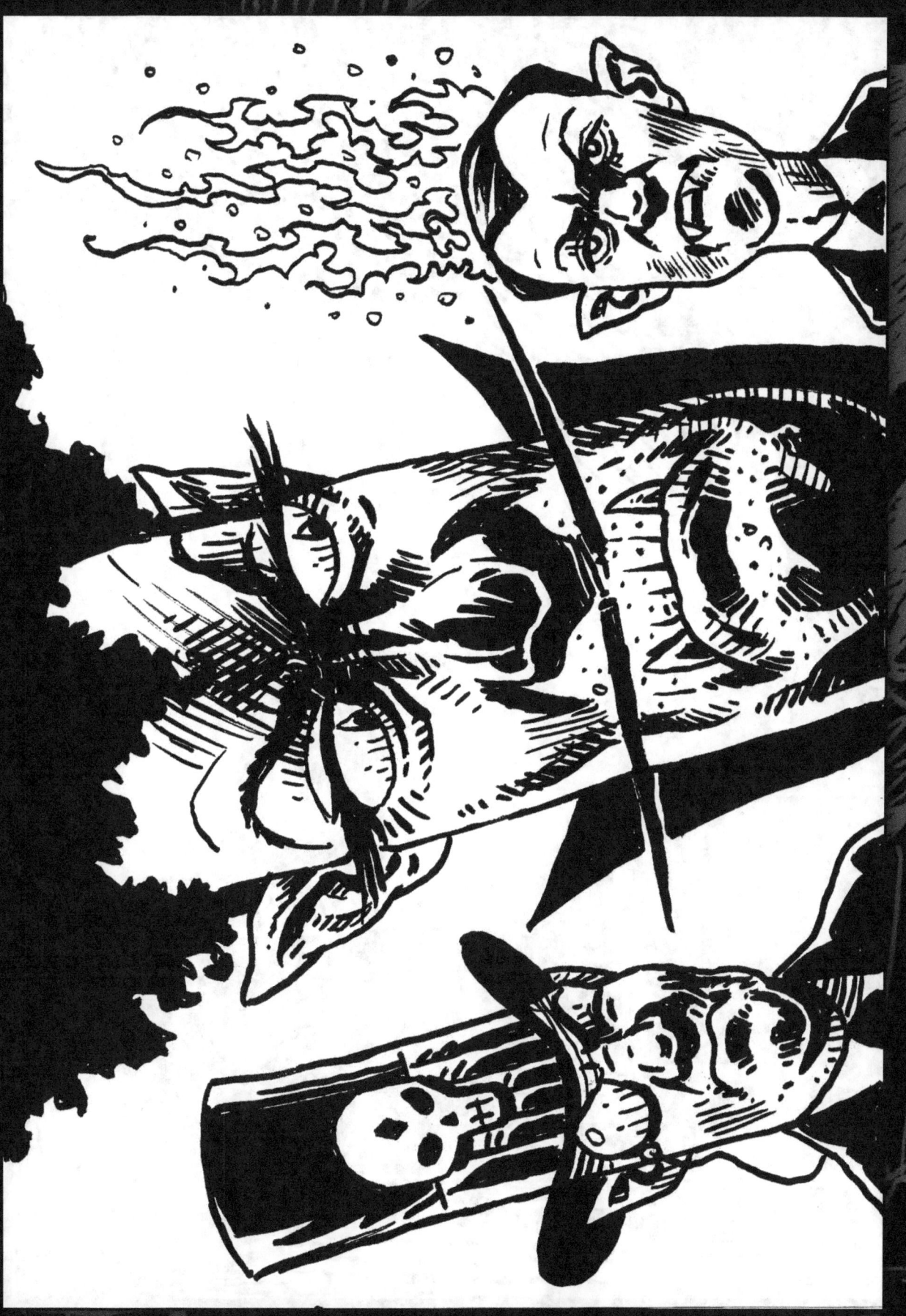

DRAC AND HIS FRIENDS

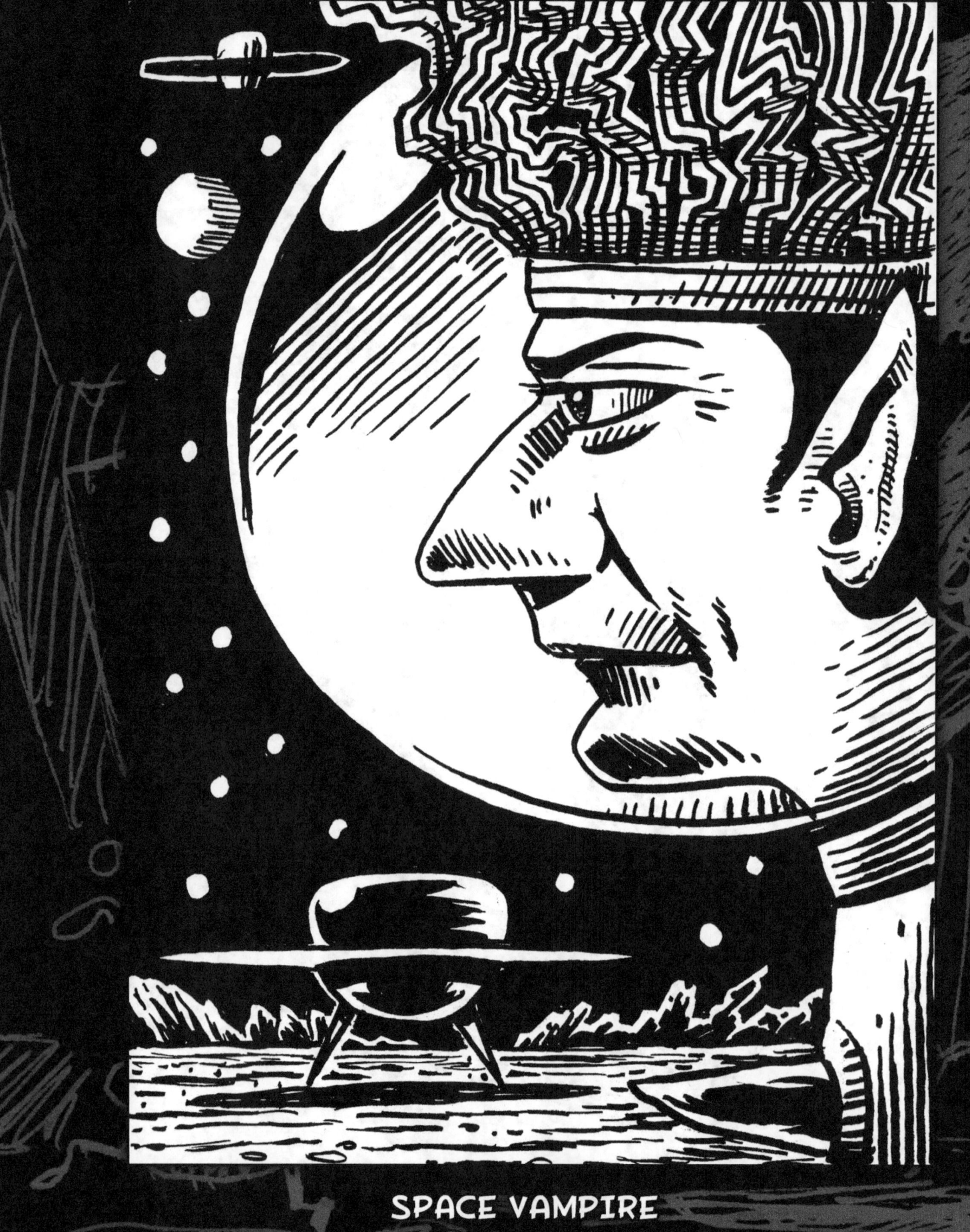
SPACE VAMPIRE

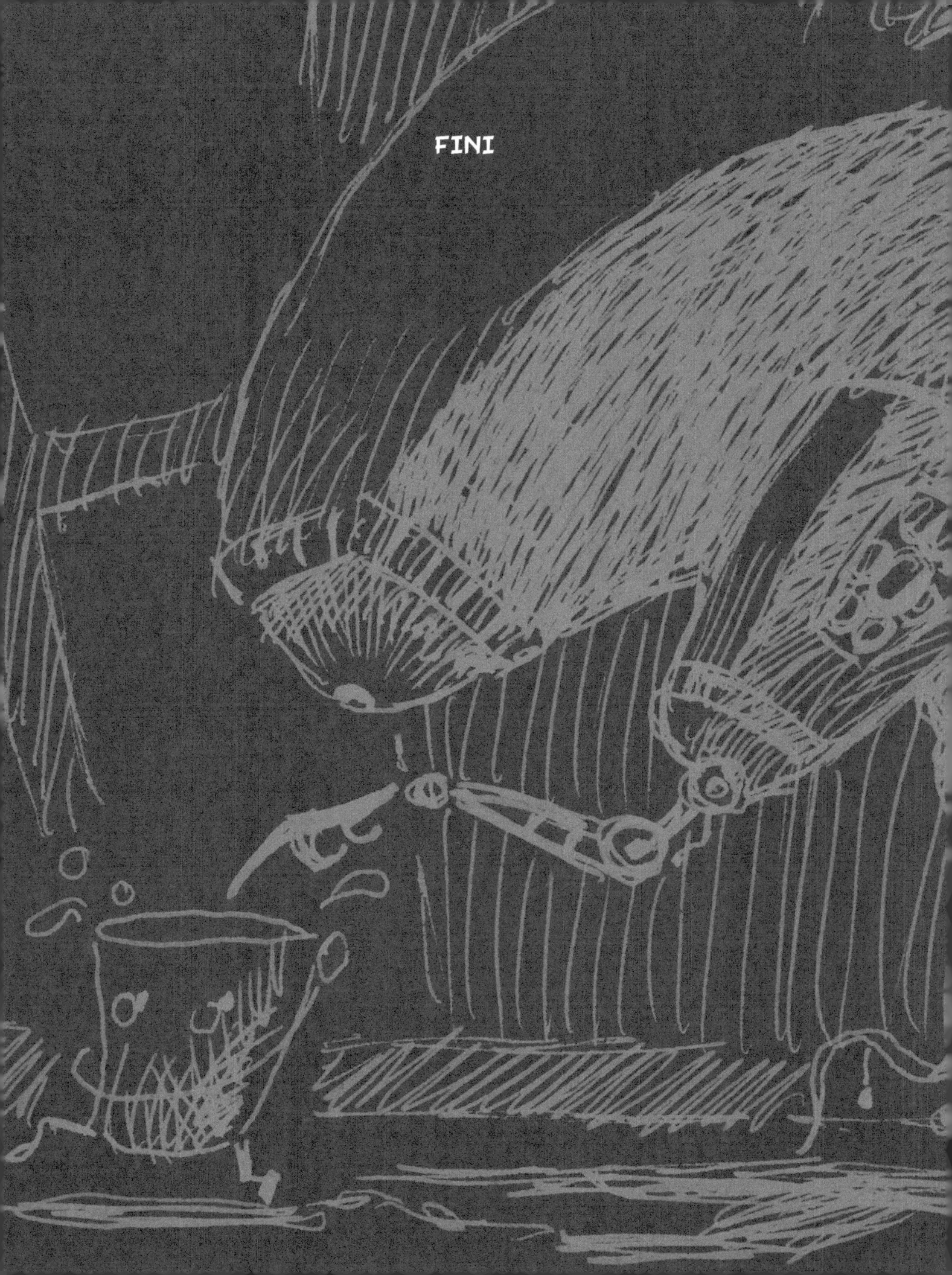

If you liked this INKTOBER pen and marker book,
you might also like the first volume of
"THE BOOK OF DOODLES"

Available on Amazon and all booksellers.

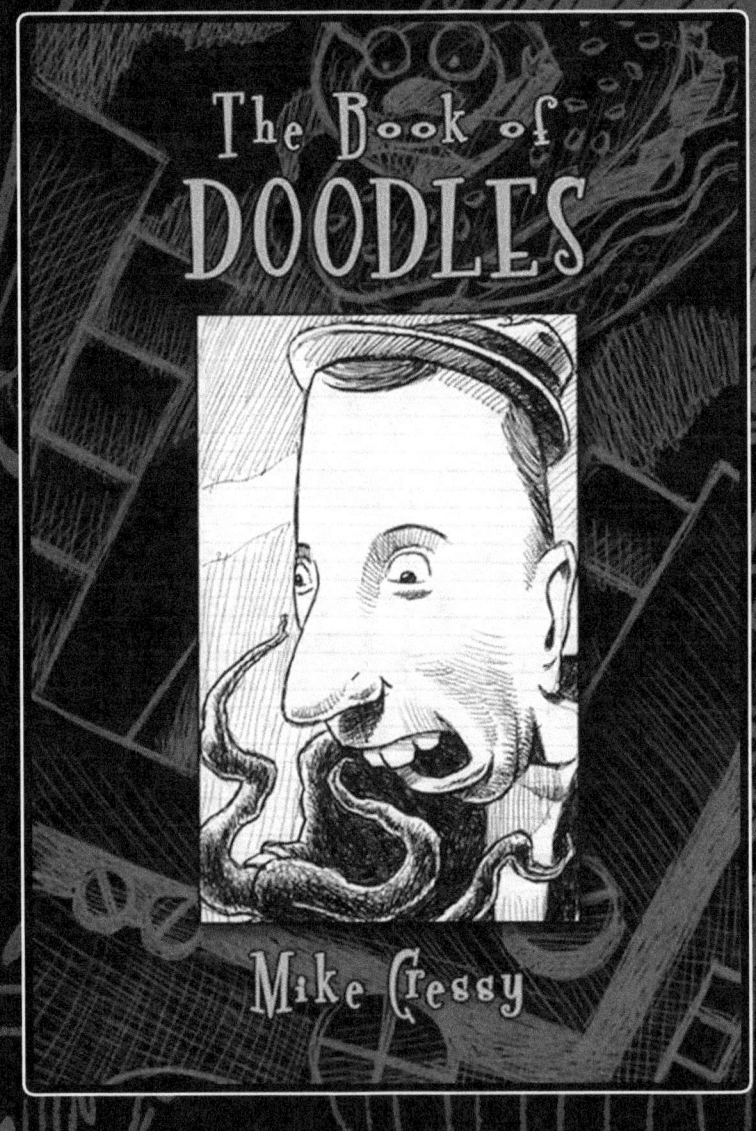

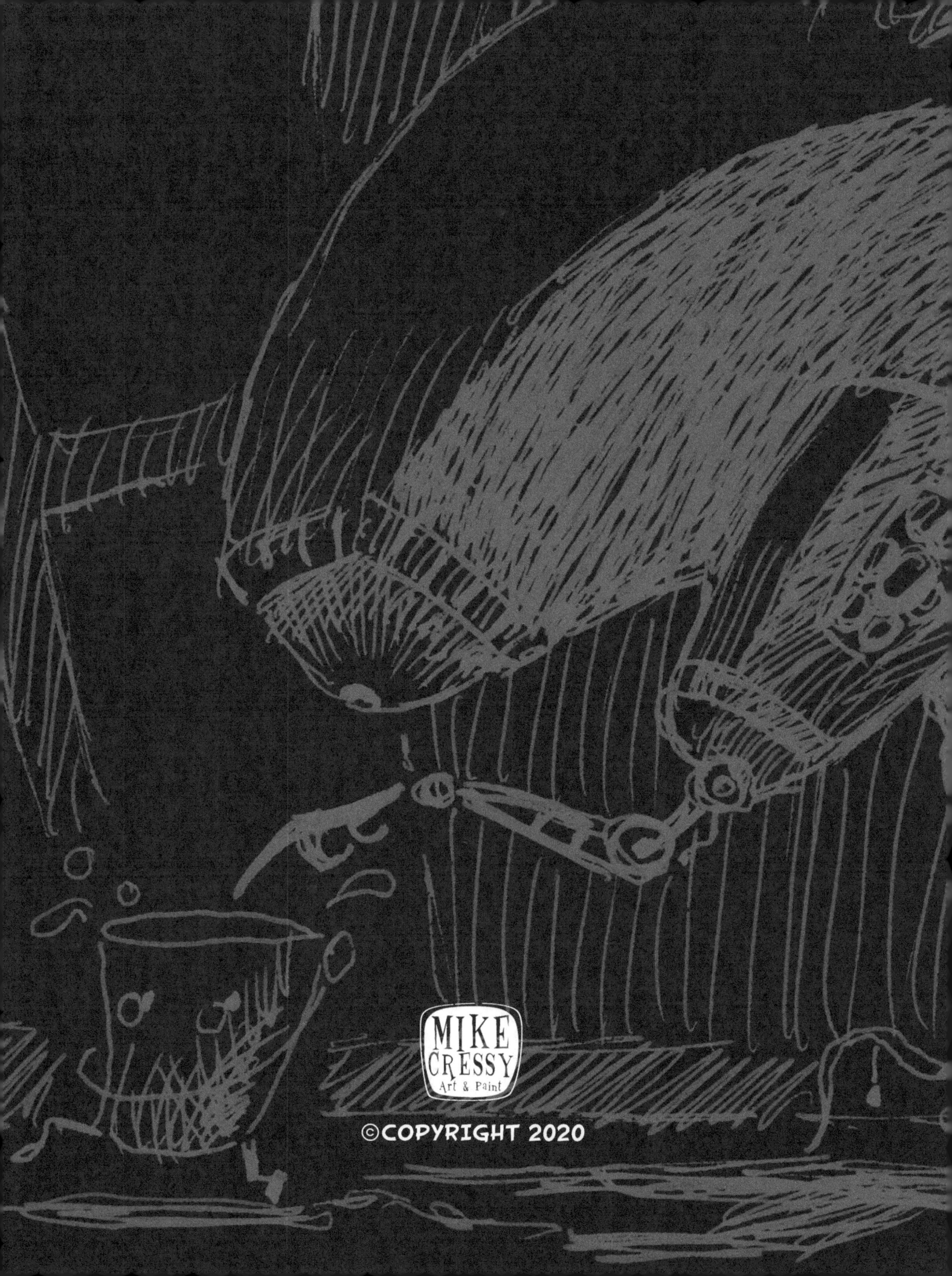

www.ingramcontent.com/pod-product-compliance
Lightning Source LLC
Chambersburg PA
CBHW082020230526
45466CB00022B/2872